THE COMPLETE GUIDE TO SELF CONFIDENCE FOR TEENS:

Empower Your Decisions, Boost Mental Well-being and Master Social Skills

AUBREY ANDRUS

CONTENTS

INTRODUCTION

Hello there, my beautiful readers! My name is Audrey Andrus, and I am thrilled to be your guide on this incredible transformative journey as we embark on our quest to be more confident and empowered individuals. I don't want you to think of me as a 35-year-old author or your run-of-the-mill motivational speaker; rather, think of me as your wingwoman who will help guide you along your way to blossom into the best versions of yourselves. With my background in life coaching and psychology, my mission is to help teens feel empowered to unlock their awesome potential and embrace their superhero force of self-worth. Through this journey, you will be exposed to some incredible actionable strategies, peppered with some relatable stories and personal tidbits, all cooked up to light that fire within you.

As we traverse the vast and intricate landscape of our teenage years, we will grow as individuals, build our self-confidence, and recognize the transformative power of the purposeful and actionable decisions we make every day. This book is more than a mere guide, but rather your trusty companion to equip you with the essential tools to effectively navigate the intricate terrain of your formative years.

As teenagers, you often stand at a crossroads of decision-making, and as you go about this era of transformation in your life, those decisions can be both thrilling and daunting. However, throughout our adventure together, I aim to instill in you the unwavering belief that your decisions possess the transformative power to help you grow into the person you wish to become by shaping your destinies with confidence and optimism. By embracing life's challenges with a confident attitude and making informed decisions to help you grow, you will unlock the potential for a future marked by success. This process lays a foundation for robust self-confidence to flourish.

Allow me to introduce an inspirational youngster I have worked closely with. Meet Dayna. She was 15 years old when I first met her, and like many teenagers, she grappled with debilitating thoughts of self-doubt as she wandered aimlessly, trying to navigate the intricate maze of adolescence. She was overwhelmed with uncertainties in her abilities and became flustered in the face of daunting decisions; thus, a shadow had been cast over her, holding her back from reaching her dreams and growing into the person she wanted to become. Dayna realized she needed to change; and approached me with her problems. Together, we forged a roadmap for her to follow to help liberate herself from self-doubt and negative thinking. Through turning challenges into opportunities, forming positive habits, setting goals for herself, learning to communicate confidently, and reinforcing her resilience, Dayna successfully navigated the complexities of adolescence and discovered her latent strength along the way. The cloud of self-doubt that had been looming over her had dissipated, and she never looked back. I love Dayna's story as it resonates with the universal struggles of teenagers, serving as a testament to the transformative journey within.

Much like Dayna, as we go on this transformative journey together, you will also delve into the essence of self-confidence, cultivate positive daily habits, conquer fear and anxiety, master confident communication, navigate social media responsibly, build resilience, set growth-oriented goals, explore your identities, foster healthy relationships, and handle inevitable conflicts and rejections.

Our teenage years are a phase marked by change, but they are also a phase in our lives brimming with opportunities to blossom and mold ourselves to become the people we want to become. We need to recognize that every decision we make, every time we socialize, and every challenge we overcome acts as a brushstroke on the canvas of the confident and empowered life we aim to forge. With that being said, I would like to extend a heartfelt welcome to all of you amazing readers as we embark on this transformative exploration together. May this journey be your guiding compass through the complexities of adolescence, offering insights that illuminate your path towards a future of resilience, authenticity, and unwavering self-belief in yourself!

THE FOUNDATION OF SELF-CONFIDENCE

Developing self-confidence is like constructing a towering building that can withstand nature's fury. The most crucial aspect for both your self-confidence and an impenetrable building is the foundation; without a strengthened foundation, everything will crumble.

Consider your foundation the layers of resilience you have attained through life's experiences. Your challenges, your victories, and even your losses. All these experiences have led to the construction of your foundation, which forms the bedrock that anchors your dreams and reinforces your mental fortitude. Now, this is no swift or easy process; like constructing a skyscraper, developing your self-confidence takes patience, perseverance, determination, and an iron will, but once all the pieces come together, you will undergo a personal transformation within yourself beyond your wildest dreams. With each challenge you overcome, your foundation will only become stronger.

WHAT IS SELF-CONFIDENCE?

I still remember my first public speaking experience in high school. Words can't describe the nerves I felt. I was so worried my classmates would judge me. I doubted my ability to express my thoughts accurately and feared being tongue-tied; however, I was determined, and despite my anxiety, I decided to confront my fear head-on. As I took to the podium, my voice was shaky and my legs were heavy. The first few moments were rough, but I found my rhythm. I couldn't believe what happened next. I was met with positive reactions and nods of encouragement from my classmates and my confidence sky-rocketed.

That day, I learned that self-confidence is not about pretending to be fearless, but rather about facing your fears courageously and acknowledging that we are more than our doubts and perceived weaknesses. That seemingly insignificant event opened my eyes to embrace challenges with a newfound confidence.

Self-confidence is a dynamic journey that lays the foundation for a more resilient, aware, and self-assured version of yourself. However, today, self-confidence has become a buzzword thrown around casually without truly understanding what it is. It is far more than a simple buzzword; it is a concept deeply intertwined with mental health and how we positively engage with the world around us. Self-confidence is responsible for shaping how we perceive ourselves, deal with challenges, interact with others, and the actions we choose to take.

Self-confidence is a way of being that allows us to know and care for ourselves. Some, like Mary Welford, describe self-confidence as being linked to our awareness and resilience in the face of challenges, while other prominent mental health figures highlight that self-confidence is practicing self-respect and courage to stand firm by our beliefs truly (Peterson, 2023).

Ultimately, self-confidence is the positive self-perception that propels courageous actions grounded in self-respect and valuing ourselves, regardless of making mistakes along the way or the status we hold. It is about embracing one's entirety, acknowledging and accepting our strengths and weaknesses.

THE DIFFERENCE BETWEEN SELF-CONFIDENCE AND ARROGANCE.

Confidence and arrogance live among a mutually shared spectrum of how we perceive ourselves and others, and how we choose to engage and portray ourselves actively. On the far end of this spectrum exists arrogance. An arrogant person is marked by an exaggerated sense of superiority. They feel the need to micromanage or control others' behaviors and feel the need to be at the center of everything. Essentially, they believe they are the best person in the room.

On the complete opposite end of this spectrum, there is self-deprecation. These individuals consistently put themselves down and downplay their abilities and accomplishments. Finally, in the middle lies self-confidence, residing in between arrogance and self-deprecation. Self-confidence can be attributed to someone who is both assertive and maintains a positive self-image. Self-confident individuals are not only keenly aware of both their strengths and weaknesses, but they also acknowledge and accept them for all they are. These individuals believe in their abilities and seek support rather than giving in to their insecurities (Cooks-Campbell, 2022).

Let's illustrate this with two high school students. One student is self-assured and assertive. They confidently and regularly lead group projects, encourage their classmates to share their ideas, and make an effort to learn about their strengths and weaknesses. This is a prime example of a confident teenager. Their confidence can be attributed to their ability to collaborate effectively with a group, value differing perspectives, and encourage constructive feedback.

Now, let's consider another high school student. When this student works on a group project, they constantly insist things go their way without considering the rest of the group's input. They refuse to seek help and collaborate with others. Furthermore, they assert their ideals forcefully on the group, blame others for setbacks, and refuse to take responsibility when they are wrong. As a result, this behavior hinders the progress and success of the project. This student is a prime example of an arrogant teenager.

The difference between confidence and arrogance is in their source of assurance. Confidence is a product of trusting yourself and recognizing that you may not necessarily possess all the tools you need to succeed while still maintaining the ability to seek support and guidance from others. In contrast, an arrogant individual will resist seeking any help as this goes against their superiority complex, thus showcasing their reluctance to acknowledge their limitations or ability to work with others. (Cooks-Campbell, 2022).

Confidence	Arrogance
Attracts people	Pushes people away
Sees criticism as a means to grow	Cannot accept criticism
Accepts responsibility	Blames others

Encourages others	Puts others down to feel better about themselves
Values the Input of Others	Has a superiority complex
Humble and willing to learn	Led by ego and refusing to be proven wrong
Aware of weaknesses	They refuse to believe they have a weakness

(Incoc, 2021)

HOW SELF-CONFIDENCE IMPACTS YOUR DAILY LIFE

Developing self-confidence will not only improve our self-perceptions but will also have a positive impact on our daily lives by shaping and elevating our actions, behaviors, and emotions. There are multiple benefits to self-confidence that impact our daily lives, such as:

- It helps us excel under pressure, and the more we develop our self-confidence, the more handling pressure begins to feel like second nature. When we enhance our self-belief in ourselves, we will be able to perform at our best more often.
- Through cultivating self-confidence, we will develop the power to influence others. Self-confidence enables us to sway and inspire others.
- Self-confidence and leadership are synonymous. When we are confident, it shows through our thoughts, behaviors, actions, posture, and voice, creating a commanding presence that helps and uplifts ourselves and others.
- Cultivating self-confidence enables us to adopt an optimistic outlook on life, as our belief in ourselves and our abilities significantly improves the more confident we are.

- With self-confidence emerges a profound sense of value within ourselves, empowering us to recognize, embrace, and celebrate our inherent self-worth.
- Through self-confidence, we develop a growth mindset and always look for ways to improve ourselves, which fosters a solid foundation for success goals, aspirations, and dreams.
- Self-confident individuals refrain from self-doubt or succumbing to negative thoughts, allowing them to break free from self-detrimental perceptions and behaviors.
- Self-confidence helps reduce anxiety and enables us to be increasingly fearless, opening doors to taking smart risks and embracing experiences beyond our comfort zones.
- Self-confidence helps liberate us from social anxiety as we become more confident, which helps us embrace our true selves without the constant stress of external judgment or the perceived need for validation.
- Adopting an optimistic outlook and being confident increases our motivation to take decisive action, which enables us to push forward and achieve our goals.
- Happiness is a frequent companion to confidence. Self-confident individuals tend to experience greater life satisfaction than those lacking confidence (North, 2023).

Knowing this, it becomes evident just how impactful self-confidence is in our daily lives, self-perception, and how we choose to see the world.

THE ROLE OF SELF-CONFIDENCE IN DECISION-MAKING

Often, self-confidence is the driving force behind effective decision-making. Confidence enables us to rely on our capabilities, make decisions that align with our principles, and face challenges head-on. Due to this, the development of self-confidence helps us elevate our capacity for decision-making by paving the way to cultivate a fulfilling and purposeful life.

Self-confidence has a profound impact on decision-making in several areas:

It Enhances our Clarity and Conviction

Confidence enables us to trust ourselves and fosters decisiveness. Through confidence, we can approach challenges with a clear understanding and align them with our values and priorities, which ensures our choices are in coherence with our authentic selves.

It Eliminates Self-Doubt

Confidence helps to dim self-doubt when faced with making a decision. It empowers us to trust our judgment and intuition; therefore, we minimize our tendency to second-guess and reduce the fear of making mistakes.

It Enables us to Take Calculated Risks

Due to diminished self-doubt, we can move beyond our comfort zones, explore new opportunities, and adopt creative solutions, which helps us formulate confident and effective decisions.

It Makes us Assertive

Self-confidence empowers us to assert our needs and opinions and set boundaries. This assertive approach increases the likelihood of voicing our opinions and advocating for our personal interests while still considering all perspectives. This leads to a more favorable and fulfilling outcome for all involved (Bradley, 2023).

THE TEENAGE BRAIN AND CONFIDENCE

Teens often struggle with developing their self-confidence, which can be attributed to the ongoing maturation of their brains. Regardless of a teenager's intelligence, they often struggle to exercise sound judgment, as this skill is still in the developmental process. While adults typically engage in the rational prefrontal cortex for decision-making and long-term consequences, teenagers typically rely on the amygdala, the part of the brain that is more emotional than rational.

The distinctive difference between the adult and teenage brains lies in the connectivity between the decision-making sector of the brain, which is still maturing in teens and may not progress uniformly. Essentially, this means that when we are overwhelmed with intense emotions, teenagers may find it challenging to articulate their thoughts in response to these overwhelming feelings. The reason is that during these moments, their actions are generally driven more by emotions than deliberate thought processes. As our brains mature, these connections strengthen, and teens gradually develop the ability to navigate and bolster their self-confidence (University of Rochester, 2022).

Furthermore, puberty marks a profound transformational period in our lives and is also when self-esteem becomes a crucial component that shapes our self-perceptions. The dynamics of social expectations, peer pressure, body image, family relationships, academic demands, and self-belief collaboratively influence our teenage self-esteem. Thus, it is paramount that we cultivate a nurturing environment that fosters self-acceptance, resilience, and reasonable expectations as we go through puberty's transformative phases (Project Red Ribbon, 2013).

NEUROPLASTICITY AND IT'S ROLE IN BUILDING CONFIDENCE

Neuroplasticity is our brain's ability to reconfigure neural connections. Neuroplasticity is especially potent in teens and offers them a beacon of hope against the intrusion of self-doubt. Neuroplasticity enables adaptation in response to new experiences, challenges, and sensory inputs. It becomes a powerful ally to help us combat self-doubt and empowers us to build and strengthen our confidence over time.

Adopt these techniques to harness neuroplasticity and bolster your confidence:

- Neuroplasticity becomes a powerful ally in combating self-doubt, empowering individuals to build and strengthen their confidence over time. Here's a straightforward guide to harnessing neuroplasticity for a confidence boost:
- Consistently reinforce your positive thoughts. Repetition of positive affirmations can gradually reshape our neural pathways associated with self-confidence
- Be aware of your negative thoughts and reshape them with positive ones, as this will help reshape our neural pathways
- Create positive mental images of success as you pursue your goals; these mental associations derive confidence and become powerful tools to achieve your goals.
- Set realistic goals and celebrate your wins. Break down your large goals into smaller, more manageable pieces. Achieving and celebrating multiple small goals helps to stimulate our brain's reward system, fostering a sense of accomplishment and confidence.
- Consistently engaging in learning; not only will this help us acquire a new skill, but it will also stimulate our

neuroplasticity by enhancing feelings of success and self-assurance.

- Exercise regularly, as this releases neurotransmitters to your brain that are associated with lifting your mood and bolstering confidence.
- Practice gratitude by expressing appreciation for the positive aspects of your life; this helps influence brain activity associated with our well-being, positive emotions, and self-confidence (Singh, 2024)

SELF-CONFIDENCE MYTHS DEBUNKED

It's no secret that confidence is regarded as one of the most universally desired psychological traits one can possess; however, there is a large disparity between the world's commonly held perceptions of confidence and the reality of this psychological trait obscured by myths. Here are five dispelled myths surrounding self-confidence.

Myth one: "Only Extroverts are Confident"

Self-confidence is not an exclusive club for extroverts; countless introverts possess quiet self-assurance. Introverts display a deep sense of self-awareness and often showcase the ability to acknowledge and appreciate their unique strengths and achievements. Confidence is far more nuanced than simply being the center of attention or the loudest person in the room. It involves a person's comfort in their own identity for all it is, be it their strengths or weaknesses, and their contentment with their own personal accomplishments, which is something both introverts and extroverts can possess (Ronin, 2020).

Myth two: "Confidence Means Never Feeling Afraid"

Feeling afraid or succumbing to insecurities occasionally does not mean that you are not confident; it means you are human. It's human nature to feel unsure of ourselves on occasion or uneasy about the unknown. Just because you may feel scared or nervous about striking up a conversation with somebody you are not entirely familiar with doesn't mean you lack confidence; it takes practice to overcome these feelings. The important thing is not letting that fear or uneasiness hold us back from becoming the person we wish to become.

Myth Three: "You're Born With Confidence"

Confidence is not a divine gift given to a chosen few at birth. It's a skill, a mindset, and an amalgamation of life experiences and exposure to different situations. People who radiate self-confidence didn't get it overnight; they worked for it, faced challenges, stretched their limits, and engaged in situations that were once out of their comfort zone. With achievable steps and a willingness to work on ourselves, anybody can be confident.

Myth Four: "Success Equals Confidence"

This myth should actually read, "Confidence equals success." More often than not, to succeed, we need to be confident first, not the other way around. You need to believe in your ability from the get-go, even if it's just a small ounce of courage to begin with. Tapping into your confidence at the start is what will lead to success. The more you succeed, the more confident you will become, but you must start working on your confidence first.

Myth Five: "Confidence is Static"

Confident people are not confident all the time. Life is a constant ebb and flow; some days, you feel invincible, and some days, doubt will creep into your mind. What's important is to get back up without letting that doubt fester. During college, I experienced highs of confidence; I felt like nothing could tear me down, but that didn't last forever. Once I graduated and entered the competitive job market, I wasn't feeling invincible, and some days I experienced self-doubt. It was uncomfortable, but I persisted. I regained my confidence through perseverance and working on myself, and I landed an amazing first job as a result.

Building a strong foundation for self-confidence is a fantastic start, but let's now explore how to strengthen that foundation daily!

DAILY HABITS FOR BUILDING CONFIDENCE

It's crucial to start the day right; after all, it sets the tone for the day. Give yourself that head start by adopting personalized morning routines to build a positive and sturdy foundation for a successful mindset to conquer the day ahead. Join me on a journey of the mundane—the magic of how our small, seemingly insignificant actions hold the key to transforming our lives for the better. Adopting positive daily routines is pivotal to our success; these habits we form orchestrate 40% of our daily actions and how we choose to live our lives (Alangui, 2022). The key to growing confidently lies in consistent, small daily actions that transform us into more confident and successful individuals.

THE IMPORTANCE OF A POSITIVE START TO THE DAY AND MORNING ROUTINES FOR CONFIDENCE

Kickstarting your day strategically with a positive outlook isn't just a mood booster; it's a game changer for mental well-being and cultivated confidence!

I make it my mission to start every morning by making myself a cup of coffee, stepping outside, breathing in the fresh air, and setting positive intentions for myself for the day ahead. This may seem simple, but this morning routine fills me with the optimism and energy I need to tackle the day to come. Now, this is just one way to do it, but there are plenty of morning routines out there that you can make your own. Choose a routine that works for you, and you'll experience a whole assortment of benefits, such as:

Mood and Confidence Boost

Employing a positive morning ritual and an optimistic headspace to start the day has been proven to uplift your mood and reinforce confidence. Not only do morning routines help us face challenges with more resilience, but studies have also shown that they help improve our relationships with ourselves and others.

Increased Productivity

Morning habits help us start the morning off feeling relaxed and energized, meaning we tend to get a lot more done. These habits will make us more productive, and studies have found that they aid individuals in approaching tasks with a clearer sense of purpose, focus, motivation, and higher performance.

Enhanced Relationships

Starting the day off right with a positive outlook radiates kindness and aids in understanding interpersonal interactions. It also helps us improve relationships with our friends, family, and classmates, and influences positive responses from those around us.

Physical Health Improvement

Research has found that starting your day with a positive mindset leads to adopting healthier habits. Whether it be a nutritious breakfast, getting regular exercise, or ensuring we get the right amount of sleep, these habits are crucial to maintaining our physical health.

Promotion of a Growth Mindset

Perhaps the most crucial aspect of starting the day with healthy habits and an optimistic mindset is that it promotes a growth mindset. By keeping up with our morning rituals, we won't only reap the benefits for one day but for days to come, too. Through consistency, we'll experience continuous improvement in effort and learning, learn from setbacks, and exhibit resilience as we tackle challenges (Fearless, 2023).

GOAL SETTING FOR THE DAY

Many people often start the day by making a to-do list. While this is a great habit to adopt, these long lists focus on too many tasks and not enough goals. Having tasks to complete is fantastic, but incorporating manageable and realistic daily goals, whether big or small, gives our daily routines a greater sense of purpose.

Daily goals are targets, ranging from ambitious aspirations to forming positive habits (Wooll, 2022). Remember, daily goals are different from long-term goals, unlike long-term goals daily goals require consistent effort and hard work on our part, but once they are achieved, it is well worth the effort.

While some goals demand time to be achieved, daily goals anchor us to the present. They help us stay productive and motivated and teach us the importance of planning (Wooll, 2022).

Daily goal setting is crucial and comes with loads of benefits.

- We spend less time procrastinating with smaller, attainable goals
- Tracking our progress becomes seamless
- We will feel a sense of obligation for each goal we set and experience satisfaction for every goal we achieve
- Daily goal setting generates momentum and will motivate us to larger, long-term goals.
- Writing down goals substantially increases the likelihood of achieving them (Wooll, 2022)

VISUALIZATION AND AFFIRMATIONS

Visualization may be a simple technique, but don't underestimate it's power. Visualization is when we form a strong mental image in our mind about a future event to make that outcome a reality (Mind Tools, 2023).

One way to make visualization part of our daily habits is to create a vision board. Recently, I've embraced this technique and created a vision board on Pinterest. Every morning, I pin images to this board. Each image represents a dream I aspire to achieve, whether scoring the winning touchdown at your football match, making tons of new friends, or becoming the next big thing in the music scene. This daily visual reminder helps me align my thoughts with my desired outcomes. They are not just images, every time I look at them, I feel the emotions tied to them and get the injection of motivation I need to make my dreams a reality.

A story that comes to mind when thinking about the power of visualization is Jim Carry's story. He wrote himself a check for 10 million dollars "for acting services rendered." The year was 1985, and he was a 23-year-old struggling actor. He wrote that $10 million check, postdated for 10 years, and every day for the next 10 years he carried it around with him as a reminder of his dream. And guess what? A decade later, he landed his first starring role in Ace Ventura, and soon after, he was cast to play the Mask. His $10 million check became a reality, and after years and years of visualization, he transformed himself from a struggling actor to the hottest comedic actor in Hollywood in the 1990s. That is the power of visualization.

However, visualization isn't the only tool we can use. Positive affirmations can be just as powerful. Affirmations are positive statements we tell ourselves to fight off any negative thoughts that might be holding us back. By saying them regularly and believing in them, we can change how we think and feel (Mind Tools, 2023).

Here are some of the morning affirmations I love to use:

- I am proud of who I am!
- I can do this, no matter what anyone says!
- I am successful!
- I am good enough!
- I am excellent at what I do!
- I am brave!
- I am strong!

- I can face any obstacle!
- I will never give up!

Combining visualization and affirmations is a powerful tool for success and a tried-and-tested method to set us up for success in the future.

MINDFULNESS AND SELF-DISCOVERY

Mindfulness is a state of being that assists us in grounding ourselves in the present. Mindfulness isn't about flicking the off switch of our thoughts entirely; rather, it is about shifting our focus to the here and now rather than on what was or what will come.

Practicing mindfulness helps us to self-reflect and, in turn, boosts our confidence in doing so. It helps us address common concerns in our lives, like stress, anxiety, and even physical pain. Furthermore, it helps improve sleep quality, assists in acquiring greater peace of mind, and helps us manage our emotions more effectively. A comprehensive analysis pulled data from 39 studies and found a noteworthy decrease in stress levels for individuals engaging in mindfulness-based interventions (Strangemore-Jones, 2024). Thus, practicing mindfulness will not only help us to live in the moment but will also make us more self-aware and confident along our journey of self-care.

MINDFULNESS EXERCISES FOR TEENS

Stress, doubt, and anxiety are, unfortunately, part of life; however, that doesn't mean we can't take action to nullify them. Every second weekend, I go hiking to get away from the stress of the weekday grind. There's something about being surrounded by chirping birds, towering trees, and the comforting embrace of nature. With every step I take, I practice mindful walking. I focus on the crunch of the leaves beneath my shoes and the rustle of the wind against the branches. These hikes have become lifelines for me; they're my sanctuary, where I can quiet my mind and reconnect with the present, leaving me refreshed and renewed for the week ahead.

Hiking isn't for everyone, but there are other mindfulness exercises you can try out for yourself:

Exercise one: Guided Meditation

Guided mediation comes with loads of benefits, such as enhanced focus, self-esteem, concentration, and memory retention. Apps like Calm and Headspace are fantastic tools that offer teens accessible guided meditation sessions to help bolster their mental well-being (Tutor Doctor, 2023).

Exercise Two: Journaling for Self-Discovery

"I can shake off everything if I write; my sorrows disappear, and my courage is reborn." Anne Frank wrote these words in her diary as she was hiding from the Nazis, emphasizing the immense power of journaling even during the most challenging of times.

Journaling becomes a doorway to self-discovery as it invites us to process and work through challenging emotions. Our journal is our sanctuary to reflect on our daily experiences, relationships, and values. It helps us deepen our connection with our thoughts and feelings. It serves as a haven for expressing complex emotions, aiding in the exploration and understanding of ourselves and the world around us in a manner that is often challenging to articulate verbally (Raypole, 2021).

Consider using some of these journaling prompts to aid you on your self-reflective journey:

Self-reflection

- What values are most important to you (honesty, compassion, etc.)? Discuss how your actions align with them.
- List three changes you have or will make to live by those values.
- "My life would be incomplete without..." Complete the sentence.
- Write about two significant life events that influenced you to become who you are today.

Difficult Emotions

- What challenging thoughts or emotions arise frequently for you?
- What emotions are hardest for you to accept? How do you handle them?
- Write about something you regret and explore the lessons you learned from it.

Journal Prompts for Love and Relationships

- Who is the person you trust most in the world, and why?
- List your strengths in relationships (loyalty, kindness, etc.).
- How do you gain strength from your loved ones?

Exercise Three: Yoga and Qigong

These two exercises are perfect for teens as they help foster creativity, enhance self-expression, and elevate body awareness. By combining breathing training and physical movement, we can alleviate stress.

Exercise Four: Mindful Walking and Hiking

Techniques like tuning into sounds and other sensory stimuli like smell as we hike or walk barefoot on a field of grass and feeling the sensation of touch with every step can enhance mindfulness. Observing the world around us and focusing on our thoughts as we walk can be a refreshing adventure. Whether you go to the park, walk on the beach, or hike an epic trail, we'll actively alleviate stress and grind ourselves in the present (Mindful Teachers, 2023).

Exercise Five: Digital Detox

This one may seem daunting, but trust me, it's liberating. Implementing a technology detox, even if it's for a day or a couple of hours, has been proven to improve our mental well-being, particularly in teens significantly. Constantly being chained to technology is proven to be a major stress factor in our lives. Having breaks from technology allows us an opportunity for instant calmness and improved control of our thoughts and emotions, as well as helping us live in the present with our friends, family, and loved ones.

Exercise Six: Morning Exercise

Starting your morning with good old-fashioned exercise isn't just a great way to get a rocking body; it's an instant mood lifter, too! Whether you decide to wake up early to pump some iron, get your blood pumping with a run, or go cycling, morning exercises release those feel-good endorphins and set a positive tone for the day (Mayo Clinic, 2020).

It's like a natural stress reliever, ensuring we face the day with confidence. Incorporating exercise into our morning routine will boost our confidence and relieve stress, make us feel relaxed, motivate us, and bolster productivity. 50% of individuals who exercise in the morning were found to have enhanced daily motivation and energy levels (Brower, 2023).

Exercise Seven: Reading Something Inspirational

Reading is self-care. It is far more than a simple pastime; it's a fantastic way to practice mindfulness, and what's more, it's enjoyable! Reading helps us nurture our mental well-being. The simple act of reading page after page helps to reduce stress, alleviate anxiety, enhance our focus, and prepare us to embrace the day ahead of us.

Reading has several benefits, making it a valuable tool in our morning routine rituals. These benefits include:

- Reading helps us ascertain a deeper understanding of our identity through self-reflection. Reading assists with memory retention and enhances cognitive function
- The more we read, the more knowledge we acquire
- Immersing ourselves in a book calms us down and helps us focus on the present
- By connecting with diverse perspectives, reading fosters empathy
- Reading requires sustained focus, thus improving our concentration.

- Reading improves our expressive capabilities through new vocabulary and narratives (Winter, 2013)

Exercise Eight: The Power of Gratitude

Gratitude is a powerful force. It grounds us in the present and forces us to appreciate what we have rather than what we don't. Gratitude is our ability to express heartfelt appreciation for life's tangible and intangible gifts.

It is an emotion consistently intertwined with our internal happiness; it nurtures our positive feelings, reinforces our appreciation of the world, and forms the foundation of healthy relationships. It is a connection to something larger than ourselves, whether to those around us, a high power, or even nature. It helps shift our focus to our blessings, thus instilling our sense of self-worth. When applied to the past, present, and future, gratitude allows individuals to savor positive memories and approach life with optimism, resilience, and confidence. (Harvard, 2021).

OVERCOMING NEGATIVE THOUGHTS

Negative thoughts often creep up on us without us even noticing it, and unfortunately, they significantly impact how we behave. These unwanted thoughts are like automatic, distorted, and unhelpful scripts that code themselves in our brains, but we can rewrite this code through awareness. Through self-awareness and identifying these negative thought patterns, we can launch our offensive against these pesky thoughts better.

There are multiple types of negative thoughts; if we can identify them, we are one step closer to irradiating them. Negative thought types include:

1. **All-or-Nothing Thinking:** believing things are either incredible or disastrous.
2. **Over-Generalization:** thinking one bad day means everything is bad.
3. **Mental Filter:** focusing on the bad aspects, even if it is only one thing, and ignoring the good. Reggie Jackson holds the record for most league strikeouts in professional baseball, but he is also considered one of the greatest baseball players of all time. Do you think he focused on the strikeouts? (Bechler, 2022)
4. **Discounting the Positive:** rejecting the good stuff as not important.
5. **Jumping to Conclusions:** manifesting negative stories without facts. This will only lead to anxiety, stress, and doubt; after all, it isn't even grounded in reality. In some cases, it can even serve as a self-fulfilling prophecy.
6. **Mind Reading:** believing you know what others are thinking negatively.
7. **Fortune Telling:** predicting the worst-case scenario as a fact.
8. **Magnifying:** making small problems seem bigger than they are.
9. **Perfectionism:** setting unrealistic standards and feeling bad if you don't meet them.
10. **Self-Putdowns:** labeling yourself with negative descriptors or blaming yourself for something that isn't your fault (Marteka, 2019).

Understanding negative thought patterns is one thing, but how do we alleviate them?

TECHNIQUES TO CHALLENGE AND CHANGE NEGATIVE THOUGHTS.

To break the cycle of negative thinking, there is a crucial technique we need to master. This skill is none other than thought reframing. By adopting this powerful trick, we can transform our perspective of the world and ourselves so that we can negate negative thoughts. It may sound cliche, but simply focusing on the positive and channeling our attention to what is going right rather than what is going wrong is the essence of thought reframing. In essence, it's turning a negative thought into a positive one.

When I am having a hectic day and drowning in tasks, I reframe my stress over what I haven't completed into gratitude for the tasks I have achieved. This subtle switch in mindset immediately boosts my optimism. Thought-refraining is a technique that cultivates gratitude. It challenges the negatives and helps us view our shortcomings as opportunities to learn, thus diminishing stress levels and promoting a calmer state of mind.

Consider these tips to practice thought reframing:

- Keep track of your negative thoughts and try to recognize a pattern
- Give yourself a break. Don't panic; pause and take a deep breath. This will help interrupt your negative thought pattern.
- Ask yourself Is it factual? Is there any logical claim to these negative thoughts? Question the truth behind your negative self-talk.
- Consider other perspectives of your negative thoughts, and don't take pessimistic thoughts at face value.
- Play a UNO reverse card and turn that negative thought into a positive or realistic counterpart.

- Practice gratitude by focusing on what you do have and not what you don't
- Seek others, like your friends and family, to gain fresh perspectives and insights that you may not have considered yourself (Calm, 2024)

BUILDING A POSITIVE SELF-TALK HABIT.

Positive self-talk is perhaps our greatest weapon against negative thinking patterns. It is an extremely powerful habit that involves fostering an inner dialogue of uplifting and positive thoughts.

It is pivotal for our mental well-being as it assists with:

- Enhancing our relationship with ourselves and others through cultivating optimism and self-assurance
- It helps mold our self-image by enhancing our self-esteem and highlighting our strengths
- It injects us with confidence in stressful and challenging situations

Consider these tips to enhance positive self-talk:

- Listen critically. In stressful situations, we are often emotionally charged and extremely harsh with ourselves. Evaluate rationally and change negative self-talk patterns.
- Create Distance. Talking to ourselves in the first person can increase our anxiety. Instead, we should speak to ourselves in the third person, as this will help regulate our emotions and view challenges as manageable.
- Tailor your self-talk to your objectives. Utilize instructional and motivational self-talk to calm yourself and instill confidence.

- Be kind to yourself. Treat yourself as a friend, you are not your own worst enemy.
- Say "I don't" instead of "I can't.". This signifies control over your actions and reinforces your determination (Psych Central, 2015).

THE ROLE OF SELF-COMPASSION

According to research, being self-compassionate is directly correlated with enhanced mental well-being (Neff, 2009). Self-compassionate individuals are generally happier, more optimistic, more curious, and more connected to themselves. It was also found that self-compassionate individuals suffered less from anxiety, depression, and the fear of failure.

A common worry among individuals is that if they are too self-compassionate, they will be lazy, complacent, and procrastinate, but that isn't true. People who are self-compassionate care deeply for their internal well-being; thus, it boosts their motivation and drives them to strive for positive change in their lives actively. Being self-compassionate means you're not being too hard on yourself when making mistakes, and as a result, you become better at learning from them to change unhelpful habits. So be kind to yourself; it makes a world of difference (Neff, 2009)!

CONQUERING SELF-DOUBT

For artists, self-doubt is common and often comes in the form of telling yourself that you're not good enough or that you'll never be as good as the artists you look up to. However, Magda Gorska, a college art student, overcame these feelings of self-doubt and conquered the pervasive specter of self-doubt. She achieved this by adopting a transformative mindset, which helped her prioritize growth as an artist over falling victim to unrealistic comparisons with others. Instead of fixating on the overwhelming standards of artists she admired, she embraced the philosophy of progress, not perfection. She identified this shift in mindset as the true measure of her success.

Throughout Magda's artistic journey, she triumphed by anchoring herself in self-honesty, goal-setting, and cultivating a supportive network. Magda emphasized the importance of staying true to yourself, setting achievable goals, and surrounding yourself with like-minded individuals radiating positive energy as the secret to success for any artist struggling with self-doubt. She understood that rejecting negativity was essential to safeguarding her artistic potential and that it was the catalyst that allowed her creativity to flourish.

Magda permitted herself to create authentically and to share her unique creations with the world, which ultimately helped her triumph as an artist. Magda's perspective on her abilities and art helped transform her life into a canvas for personal expression, emphasizing that her creative journey was not a spectator sport but an ongoing exploration for her to discover (Skill Share, 2024).

With a positive mindset, the next task on our agenda is to tackle barriers that could potentially hold us back!

CONQUERING FEAR AND ANXIETY

S tudies by the National Institute of Mental Health and the Child Mind Institute found that 31.9% of teenagers grapple with some anxiety disorder.

Stress, fear, and anxiety are complex realms, and in the pages to follow, we will explore the path toward conquering our fears and anxieties.

IDENTIFYING SOURCES OF FEAR AND ANXIETY

We all get anxious and scared; it's just part of life; however, what causes these emotions is crucial to effectively dealing with them. Once we pinpoint the cause, we can adopt a solid starting point to find solutions to the deeper problems. This awareness empowers us to take actionable steps and make positive changes to overcome our fears and anxieties.

When I was in high school, I suffered from a lot of anxiety. For a while, I didn't understand it, but after some time, I realized I was holding myself back due to the fear of not fitting in at school and meeting the social expectations I had set for myself. Through identifying the cause, I took actionable steps like being more self-compassionate, being more authentic, re-evaluating my expectations of myself, going out to seek like-minded friends, and joining the softball club after school. Understanding the source of my anxiety helped me work through my fears and anxieties and take action to overcome them.

Now, not everybody will struggle with the same fear, but you may be feeling anxiety for all sorts of other reasons. Consider these common anxieties and triggers that teenagers face to help you identify what is causing your anxiety:

- Relationship Problems
- Public Speaking
- Meeting new people and Striking conversations with unfamiliar people
- Social expectations and peer pressure
- Self-esteem and confidence issues
- Academic expectations and performance
- Comparing ourselves to others on Social Media and cyberbullying
- Family conflict and unrealistic expectations
- Body image concerns
- Uncertainty about the future (Sedona Sky Academy, 2024)

THE DIFFERENCE BETWEEN FEAR AND ANXIETY

On the surface, fear and anxiety may seem and even feel the same, but the way we respond to these emotions is quite fundamentally different. Fear is a response to an immediate threat and requires swift action. When we experience fear, a psychological response known as "fight or flight" is triggered, prompting us to either prepare to confront danger or flee from it. Fear leads to heightened senses and quick decision-making.

In contrast, anxiety is a prolonged fear. Anxiety does not prompt us to take immediate action; rather, it makes us dwell on potential dangers, even if they are nonexistent. This often leads to tensed muscles, racing thoughts, and a struggle to feel at ease. Think of anxiety as a pesky and persistent voice whispering worry and distress in our ears, leading to avoidance behaviors and reluctance to face challenges head-on (Mclean Hospital, 2023).

For instance, if we were walking in a tranquil forest but suddenly heard a rustle in the bushes, fear would prompt us to take immediate action—surveying for threats; perhaps the rustle was caused by a wild animal. In an instant, almost reflexively, we would decide whether to stand our ground (fight) or swiftly leave for safety (flight). On the other hand, if we experienced anxiety, we would be frozen in our tracks and avoid taking immediate action. Even after the rustling stops, the feeling of uneasiness will persist. This would create ongoing concern for the remainder of the walk and future walks. Fear is a reflex for immediate safety, while anxiety lingers, influencing daily life.

THE ROLE OF STRESS IN FEAR AND ANXIETY

Stress, anxiety, and fear go hand in hand; it's like a toxic relationship. When an individual experiences stress, anxiety symptoms are triggered, and as a result, individuals will experience heightened stress and prolonged fear responses. The interconnectedness of these emotions amplifies a cycle in which our overall mental well-being is negatively impacted. Teenage stress is prevalent today, be it from social, academic, self-esteem, or body image stressors. These stressors act as catalysts for various negative behaviors, such as avoidance behaviors, lashing out, and rebelling.

Understanding that anxiety and fear are integral parts of the cycle of stress indicates the need to adopt comprehensive approaches to managing our stress to foster our inner resilience and promote a healthier approach to managing our daily challenges (Iliades, 2018).

TECHNIQUES FOR TRACKING AND UNDERSTANDING YOUR ANXIETY

Exploring the depth of our anxieties requires us to take a proactive approach to introspection and mindfulness. This will help us enhance our understanding of ourselves and assist us in tracking and decoding our anxieties.

Consider these tips to get a better grasp on your anxiety:

- Name your anxiety. Begin by identifying and verbalizing what your anxiety is in different scenarios. This helps promote emotional acknowledgment and self-awareness.
- Set some time aside every day to document your anxieties in a journal and uncover their origins. This will help us find patterns and clarity.
- Focus on the specifics. Select a chosen anxiety, note its triggers, its frequency and intensity, and try to notice patterns. For example, is it worse at a specific time of the day, or are there certain things you can avoid being triggered by?
- Expand your emotional vocabulary. Use diverse words to describe how you are feeling. For instance, how many words can you use to describe feeling frustrated? Agitated, annoyed, discontented, vexed, irritated, etc. This will help enhance our comprehension of how we are feeling. (Buckloh, 2018).

STRATEGIES FOR FACING YOUR FEARS

Embracing our fears head-on is not only courageous but crucial for personal growth. Together, we will discover the tried and tested strategies to cultivate our resilience and propel us on a path of self-discovery, putting us one step further toward our journey of inner strength and confidence.

Exposure Therapy

Exposure therapy has proven to work wonders for a host of anxiety disorders. It is a psychological technique that helps individuals address their anxieties and combat avoidance behaviors. In essence, it involves facing situations head-on that you are uneasy with or scared to disrupt avoidance tendencies. While avoiding situations that frighten us may bring temporary relief, it can significantly enhance our feelings of fear in the long run. For that reason, psychologists use exposure therapy to help individuals overcome their fears in a supportive environment where they can safely confront their fears.

Exposure therapy utilizes different approaches to cater to individual needs.

1. **In vivo exposure:** taking the bull by the horns and facing our fears in real life. For instance, public speaking can be used to address social anxiety.
2. **Imaginal exposure:** using mental imagery to face our fears.
3. **Virtual reality exposure:** using VR to create a virtual simulation of our anxiety. For instance, somebody who is anxious in large crowds can be thrown into a virtual simulation of a crowd that gradually gets larger and larger (American Psychological Association, 2022).

Axel's Journey With Exposure Therapy

Axel was a high school junior who regularly got good grades, yet despite this, he found himself struggling with paralyzing anxiety as he feared judgment from his classmates and battled with perpetual feelings of social inadequacy. This made routine tasks feel daunting and seemingly insurmountable for him.

Axel decided to be proactive and sought out help from a residential treatment center where he would undergo exposure therapy to help him overcome his fears and anxieties. Slowly but surely, Axel tackled his anxieties methodically, conquering what held him back one task at a time. This empowered Axel to confront and master his fears, which progressively led to his desensitizing himself from their impact.

He would be thrown into the deep end by enduring social simulations and public speaking to help him overcome his fear of social judgment and his perceived notion that he wasn't as good as his peers. With the help of exposure therapy, Axel gained crucial coping mechanisms, resilience, and emotional control to manage his anxiety. Today, as a college freshman, Axel confidently navigates social interactions with determination and resilience, underscoring the significance of effectively addressing anxiety for a brighter future (Yin, 2017).

Small, Manageable Steps to Overcome Your Anxiety

While exposure therapy is a wonderful form of therapy, it won't work for everyone, and not everybody will be comfortable trying it either. Have you ever heard the saying, "How do you eat an elephant? One bite at a time, that's how." That same sentiment applies to facing our anxieties. Sometimes, the best way to overcome anxiety is to break down what is making us anxious into small, bite-sized steps that we can sequentially and systematically achieve to ultimately overcome our anxiety and bolster our confidence along the way.

Follow these steps to help you overcome your anxiety steadily yet effectively:

1. **Define your goal:** What is your end game? Will overcoming this anxiety help you be calmer, reclaim control of your life, or boost your confidence? Whatever the goal, identifying it helps set a foundation for managing our anxiety more effectively.
2. **Break it down:** Focusing on achievable tasks gradually reduces anxiety, bringing a sense of accomplishment and control to our journey.
3. **Visualize the journey:** Create visual roadmaps, a journal, and use mind maps to document your progress. This shows a trend of growth and will keep us motivated on our journey, in addition to allowing us to identify and manage concerns effectively.
4. **You're not alone:** If you are ever feeling overwhelmed, don't be afraid to share your feelings with your support system, whether it be your friends, family, psychologist, or anybody else you trust.
5. **Set achievable and realistic milestones.** Establish benchmarks with manageable steps and deadlines to achieve them (Leal, 2021).

Through adopting incremental steps, overcoming a challenge becomes less daunting and often more effective as it feels more realistic and achievable. As we progress through this journey, we can observe our growth and gradual erosion of resistance to change along the way, leading us on a more confident path! (Calm, 2023)

Don't Underestimate Small Wins!

Breaking down our fears into small, manageable steps also means we will be celebrating loads of small victories. Don't underestimate small wins; it's the little things that lead to success at the end of the day. When we recognize and celebrate these milestones, we enhance our self-confidence, motivate ourselves to overcome challenges, and make steady but monumental progress toward our end goals. Small wins give us the momentum and energy we need to trudge forward with the optimism and "can-do" attitude we need to overcome our anxieties.

Follow these tips to celebrate more regularly:

- Define what small wins mean to you and only you. It doesn't matter what others think.
- Diligently track your progress
- Set realistic and manageable steps to win
- Don't be afraid to reward yourself and others for your achievements.

With small wins, we cultivate an environment of resilience, optimism, and a sense of fulfillment for ourselves as we march forward on our journey of growth and success (Gasparinetti, 2023).

The Role of Support Systems

Teenagers are still forming their identities and are at a vulnerable time in their lives. A solid support system helps them find themselves and feel better mentally and emotionally. A support system can comprise anybody—friends, family, teachers, boyfriends, girl-friends, sports coaches, therapists, you name it. Their influence is monumental; it provides teens with practical help and support to help them through tough times. A support group is like a safety net that catches you when you most need it and supports you even if you aren't aware of it.

However, a support group is more than just a group of people who help you deal with your problems. They make teens feel like they matter like they belong to something; knowing that they are part of a group where they are cared for and respected boosts their confidence, making them extremely valuable (Liu et al., 2021).

YOUR GO-TO "ANXIETY TOOLKIT"

Anxiety can be an unpredictable beast and can strike at any moment, leading us to feel overwhelmed with a feeling of unease that permeates our thoughts and emotions. Luckily, there are techniques we can use to manage our anxiety and bring quick relief in moments of uneasiness.

Tool One: Breathing Techniques for Immediate Relief.

Breathing techniques are powerful weapons in times when anxiety strikes. Using mindful breathing is highly effective in bringing about a sense of calm during times of heightened anxiety. Whether it be to calm your nerves right before an exam or to find your rhythm in a stressful social setting, these breathing techniques can significantly combat feelings of anxiety. Utilize these breathing techniques to regain your composure when you find yourself in a stressful situation.

1. **2-to-1 breathing:** Exhale for twice as long as you do inhaling; repeat this until you feel a sense of calm.
2. **Boxed breathing:** Inhale for four seconds, then hold that breath in for four seconds. Then exhale and hold that

exhaled breath for four seconds before inhaling again and starting the process all over again.

3. **Alternate-nostril breathing:** Pinch one nostril closed while you inhale deeply with your other nostril, then switch the nostril you are holding and exhale from the other nostril. (Tutor Doctor, 2023)

Tool two: The 5-4-3-2-1 Technique

This technique is simple but crucial to help disrupt anxious thoughts and ground us in the present moment. This technique forces us to engage with all five senses. We start by naming five things we can see (desk, pencil, highlighter, calculator, cellphone, etc.), which help disrupt our negative thought patterns. Next, we close our eyes and identify four sounds (the wind rustling, birds chirping, cars driving, rain, etc.). This redirects our focus outwardly. Following this, we concentrate on three things we can feel (the ground beneath our feet, the wind on our necks, the fabric of our clothes on our skin, etc.), thus connecting us to our immediate surroundings. Next, we need to identify two smells (lavender in the air, the aroma of coffee, etc.) This anchors us in the present moment. Lastly, we need to focus on taste, such as the taste of our saliva. Ultimately, this exercise helps us face and manage our emotional responses to a situation and instills a sense of calm (Calm, 2023a).

Tool Three: Visualization for Calm

Visualization is a technique we can use not only to manifest our futures but also as a potent anxiety-relief technique. It utilizes mental imagery to induce a state of relaxation and calm. Visualization helps us tap into our imaginations and proves an effective weapon for redirecting negative and anxious thoughts into more optimistic and constructive ones.

Before we use visualization, we must create a comfortable environment for ourselves free from distractions. Once you have created that space, choose a comfortable position to either sit or lie down in, and remove restrictive clothing or accessories.

Here's a brief visualization technique I love to do:

- **Step 1:** Envision yourself in a tranquil garden setting
- **Step 2:** Immerse yourself in the garden with calming elements

  - The garden's vibrant colors, stunning trees, and blooming flowers
  - The sound the wind makes as the leaves sway in the breeze
  - The aroma of the flowers
  - The warmth of the sunlight as it hits your skin
  - The soothing sound of the garden fountain and the birds chirping in the trees

- **Step 3:** Release any tension you feel in your face and let go of the stress in your forehead, your eyebrows, your throat, and your neck
- **Step 4:** Sync your breathing with the natural rhythm of your imagined garden atmosphere
- **Step 5:** Embrace the tranquility of the gardens and feel yourself connecting with nature

As you finish this visualization exercise, slowly open your eyes, knowing you can return to this serene mental haven whenever you are feeling overwhelmed to find relief in moments of anxiety. (Star, 2019).

Tool Four: Physical Exercise

Exercise can work wonders to get rid of debilitating anxious thoughts. Setting aside to go on a bike ride, dance your stress away, or run around the block is beneficial for individuals struggling with anxious thoughts.

Why? Well, here's your answer:

- It's a distraction; exercising redirects our focus from anxious thoughts to our body's movement.
- Moving our body helps relieve muscle tension, thus alleviating our body's physical contribution to anxiety.
- It improves our psyche; our increased heart rates trigger the release of anti-anxiety neurochemicals such as serotonin, endocannabinoids, GABA, and BDNF.
- It triggers frontal brain activation. When we exercise, we activate our frontal brain, which is responsible for regulating the amygdala's response to perceived threats (Ratey, 2019).

Tool Five: Manage Social Media Time

Managing the amount of time we spend on social media can profoundly impact how we manage our stress levels. Excessive use of social media often induces stress. This stress isn't only attributed to the content we consume, but also because we could have used that same time to connect with friends, engage in outdoor activities, and spend our time on more constructive actions to enhance our mental and emotional well-being. What's more, using social media at night can further exacerbate stress, as this hinders our ability to wind down at night, essentially resulting in a reduction in the quality and duration of adequate rest.

Tool Six: Connecting With Others

We are social creatures, so establishing connections with others is paramount to managing and reducing stress, and promoting our overall well-being. Building a sense of belonging provides us with invaluable support, companionship, and a sense of belonging. These connections will not only reduce our stress levels but will also serve as a source of encouragement during challenging times (Hesler, 2023).

We've managed to keep our anxiety in check, but now we need to master how we interact with others!

MASTERING SOCIAL SKILLS

Have you ever wondered why some people make forging connections with others seem effortless? Well, it's not just about confidence; it is through their determination to practice and master their communication and listening skills and understand the importance of nonverbal cues. Building and nurturing connections takes time and persistence. Once we get the hang of it and hone our communication skills, our self-confidence and self-awareness will drastically improve and leave lasting positive impressions on others.

NON-VERBAL COMMUNICATION

We cannot undermine the significance of the role non-verbal communication plays in the overall effectiveness of communication. Studies have shown that up to 65% of our daily interactions can be attributed to non-verbal communication (Cherry, 2023a). This is facilitated through facial expressions, hand gestures, eye gaze, posture, personal space, and tone.

Understanding non-verbal communication in our daily social inter-actions is crucial, as it plays an integral role in effective communica-tion, such as:

- Forming a foundation of trust. Maintaining eye contact, nodding while others speak, and subconsciously mirroring other people's body language signifies a bond of connection and builds trust.
- Emphasizes what we are trying to convey. The tone of our voice, hand gestures, and how we adopt spatial awareness influence how our message will be received and can accentuate certain points.
- It reveals hidden truths. When there is a disconnect between our verbal and non-verbal communication, it may indicate that we are hiding something and being dishonest, allowing us to read intuitively between the lines.
- It reveals our true feelings. When we monitor body language, such as a clinched jaw, darting eyes, or slumped posture, we can recognize the real emotions people are experiencing, just by looking at them (Cherry, 2023a).

Thus, it is evident that non-verbal cues convey vital information that transcends spoken words.

UNDERSTANDING BODY LANGUAGE

To truly grasp non-verbal communication, we need to ascertain a holistic understanding of non-verbal cues as a collective and acknowledge the contextual factors behind these cues to fully comprehend their interpretation.

Facial Expressions

Our faces contain immense communication potential through their expressions. A smile can convey happiness, satisfaction, or approval, while a frown often signals disappointment or sadness.

Our facial expressions hold many secrets and often reveal our genuine feelings. We can tell a lot through our facial expressions; we can deduce emotions such as surprise, fury, joy, disgust, anxiety, confusion, fear, focus, desire, and contempt just by looking at someone's face. Additionally, our facial expressions can make us more approachable and influence our perceptions of trustworthiness. You are far more likely to approach somebody with a friendly facial expression than a hostile one; furthermore, you will most likely trust somebody who seems calm more than if they display nervousness.

The Eyes

The eyes are the window to the soul and provide invaluable insight into a person's true feelings and thoughts. Take notice of eye movements, such as direct eye contact, darting eyes, reluctance to meet your gaze, pupil dilatation, and blinking habits. Direct eye contact indicates that somebody is interested in what you are saying, while someone averting your gaze can indicate discomfort or distraction. Darting eyes can convey nervousness or distrust, while extreme, frequent blinking habits can indicate that someone is lying. Diluted pupils can sometimes indicate attraction or arousal (Cherry, 2023a).

The Mouth

Often overlooked are the telltale signs our mouths convey. If you see somebody chewing on their bottom lip, this may indicate they are worried, insecure, or fearful. Covering our mouths with our hands, excluding coughing and yawning, could indicate disgust, shock, or disapproval. Smiles can indicate that we are happy, but they can also show that we are being cynical or malicious. Pursed lips can indicate distrust or disapproval. So, be wary of people's mouths, as they can reveal hidden truths.

Gestures

Gestures have universal and cultural variations and are a key component of body language. Waving, pointing, and finger gestures convey distinct meanings but also hold cultural nuances and may be misinterpreted based on culture. For instance, a clenched fist can indicate hostility, but, it can also indicate solidarity when punched in the air after an achievement. The "okay sign" (a circle created by touching the thumb and index finger together while extending the remaining three fingers) often indicates that everything is alright. However, in some countries in Europe, it can be used to imply that somebody means nothing, while in some regions of South America, it is a vulgar symbol. Making a V shape with our fingers can indicate victory; however, that gesture with the back of our hands facing outwards is disrespectful in the UK and Australia. While hand signals are a great way to accentuate our points, awareness of cultural differences is essential for accurate interpretation (Cherry, 2023a).

Our Arms and Legs

When we cross our arms, it can convey defensiveness, while crossing our legs and pointing them away from somebody can indicate discomfort or dislike. Rapidly tapping our fingers on a surface or fidgeting with our fingers may signify nervousness and restlessness, while standing with our hands on our hips can show confidence or aggression. Clasping our hands behind our backs can indicate that we are either bored or nervous. Thus, the positioning of our arms and legs can convey a wealth of information to others.

Posture

How we present ourselves through our posture can convey a lot about our true feelings and personality traits. A closed posture, such as slouching and crossing our arms and legs to hide the trunk of our body, can indicate tiredness, anxiety, a lack of self-confidence, hostility, and unfriendliness, making us less approachable.

In contrast, open posture is when the trunk of our body is open and exposed while keeping our backs straight and our shoulders pushed back. This indicates confidence, friendliness, openness, and willingness, making us more approachable.

Personal Space

Respecting people's personal space is non-negotiable; it can make people feel uncomfortable, threatened, imposed upon, and disrespected. Edward T. Hall, an anthropologist, coined the term proxemics, which refers to the distance between people when they interact. He broke down proxemics into four distances based on social interactions: intimate, personal, social, and public proxemics.

Intimate distance (6 to 18 inches) implies a romantic relationship or a close relationship with people we feel incredibly comfortable with. While personal (1.5 to 4 feet) and social (4 to 12 feet) distances will vary based on the degree of comfortability and familiarity we have with a person. Public distance (12 to 25 feet or more) is typical when giving a presentation in class or in public speaking situations. Our personal space is vital to assessing the level of comfort we have with others and whether that comfortability is reciprocated (Cherry, 2023a).

LISTENING SKILLS

Communication requires listening, but here's the strange part: given how much listening we do in our daily lives, we'd be good at it, right? Well, unfortunately, that's not the case. According to research, we only recall 25–50% of what has been communicated to us (Mind Tools, 2022). For instance, in a 10-minute conversation with a friend, the majority of people will completely miss over half of that exchange of information.

We use listening to obtain information, to understand, and to learn. These are crucial elements in supporting effective communication. While listening doesn't come naturally to most of us, we can improve this skill by practicing and refining it with techniques and exercises (Mind Tools, 2022).

THE IMPORTANCE OF ACTIVE LISTENING

Active listening is the bedrock of effective and confident communication. It is a technique used to engage with someone who is communicating with you fully. It not only helps in showing and gaining understanding, but it also assists with respectful and relevant responses.

Through active listening, we foster mutual understanding, reduce conflict, and build connections. To master this technique, we need to provide our undivided attention to the speaker, provide them with feedback, resist judgment, and elicit thoughtful responses. In essence, active listening enhances genuine connections and cultivates meaningful communication. Through practicing active listening, we become better communicators, persuaders, and influencers, thus improving our ability to foster meaningful relationships (Mind Tools, 2022).

In high school, my group and I were given a challenging group project. We were tasked with creating a sustainable community garden, and as expected, there were diverse ideas among our group, and differing methods sparked tension. We weren't making progress, and then we realized we weren't truly listening to one another. We decided to use active listening; instead of arguing, we offered genuine feedback; we resisted judging differing ideas; and, like magic, we managed to transform conflicting ideas into a cohesive strategy we could all get behind. Not only did this get us a fantastic grade, but it also improved our teamwork and strengthened our friendship. Active listening assists us in truly hearing one another and steering away from impulsive responses. It transforms conflict into collaboration.

TECHNIQUES FOR ACTIVE LISTENING:

Active listening may sound difficult at first, but it is a lot easier than you may think if you make use of these techniques:

Stay Focused

- Provide your undivided attention.
- Resist preparing responses in your head.

- Take note of non-verbal cues (Mind Tools, 2022).

Illustrate That You Are Listening

- Use non-verbal cues to show engagement (Nod, smile, and, maintain an open posture)
- Switch your gaze between their eyes and mouth every few seconds.
- Avoid fidgeting
- Use verbal comments like "uh-huh" and "I see" to show that you are listening.

Provide Feedback and Gain Understating

- If you are still confused, paraphrase to ensure your understanding. Start your response with, "It sounds like you are saying..."
- Ask follow-up questions.
- Summarize the speaker's comments.

Refrain From Judgment and Interruption

- Let the speaker finish speaking before you respond.
- Avoid counterarguments while they are still speaking.
- Avoid emotional reactions
- Don't assume or predict what they will say next

Respond Appropriately

- Be respectful yet assertive with your responses
- Be honest, open, and candid when you respond
- Use open-ended questions to encourage understanding and further expression (British Heart Foundation, 2018).

EMPATHETIC LISTENING

Similarly, with active listening comes empathetic listening; while they are similar, they are different. Empathetic listening is highly effective in fostering genuine communication and connections. Simply put, this technique revolves around our ability to be attentive and responsive to others during a conversation. It enables us to build emotional connections, find similarities between experiences, and offer heartfelt responses without providing advice or criticism; instead, we focus on offering support.

So how do we do it? Here's how:

Create a Comfortable Space

- Find a quiet and safe environment conducive to open discussion
- Limit distraction by turning off your devices and speaking in private

Acknowledge Their Feelings

- Wholeheartedly acknowledging the speaker's emotions without judgment.
- Show that you understand by using phrases like "I hear you."

Watch for Body Language

- Look for signs of discomfort or nervousness, like fidgeting, darting eyes, or closed posture.
- Respond with an open posture and speak calmly.

Let Them Control the Conversation

- Don't rush them. Let them share their feelings at their own pace
- Let them end and begin discussions on their terms and show respect if they need to take breaks

Don't Interrupt

- Resist sharing your opinions unless it is asked of you
- Make use of active listening and utilize small verbal and non-verbal acknowledgments. This could be a small nod or simply saying, "I understand."

Be Encouraging

- Offer positive reinforcement when appropriate.
- Make use of positive affirmations and acknowledge that you believe in their ability to handle challenges (Indeed, 2023).

COMMON LISTENING ERRORS

As I said earlier, you'd think that based on how much listening we do in our daily lives, we'd be good at it, but that isn't the case. Take note of these listening mistakes that often hold us back:

Error One: Being Distracted

Due to the fast-paced world we live in, we all fall victim to this common listening mistake. Luckily, the solution to avoiding being distracted while communicating is rather simple. We need to resist the urge to multi-task and acknowledge that the person we are communicating with deserves our full attention. Making use of active listening will help you avoid this common listening mishap.

Error Two: Impatience

Impatience can hinder effective communication. Instead of rushing from one point to the next, slow down and hit the brakes. Let others express themselves fully before you respond. By pausing and valuing their perspective, the conversation can play out far smoother in a more respectful and collaborative exchange of ideas.

Error Three: Filtered Listening

A common trap is allowing our past experiences to shape our interpretation of a conversation. To overcome this, practice going into a conversation with an open mind, resisting the urge of previous experiences to dictate your expectations, and embracing a conversation with a clean slate void of prejudice.

Error Four: Selected Listening

This is when we only hear what we want to hear based on external factors. Perhaps we feel superior to others, or we feel they tend to fabricate the truth. Regardless, effective listening requires us to offer equal attention to everyone, irrespective of their identity or status (Rosen, 2019).

EXERCISES TO IMPROVE LISTENING SKILLS

Practice makes perfect, right? Now that we're aware of the magic of listening, let's spice things up and sharpen our skills with these exercises.

1. **Don't forget the lyrics:** For this exercise, simply choose a song to jam to, listen to it once or twice, and then try to replicate the lyrics on a blank piece of paper. Compare the lyrics you wrote down to the actual song and see how well you did.
2. **Draw a story:** Pair up with a friend and ask them to write a short story and read it to you. They can only read the story to you once, so you need to draw out that story and see if you have all the important details.
3. **Pop Quiz:** Find a song, story, poem, or podcast, listen to it once, and challenge a friend who's heard it before to create a quiz for you to complete. Fill in the blank space with your answers and see how well you retained the content.

These exercises are designed to enhance your focus, eliminate distractions, and improve your capacity to effectively retain and respond to information (Grade University, 2023).

SPEAKING WITH CONFIDENCE

 "It took me quite a long time to develop a voice, and now that I have it, I am not going to be silent."

— MADELEINE ALBRIGHT

The key to speaking with confidence is finding your voice. It's the secret sauce to a successful recipe of social expression and confidence. Finding it helps us feel empowered, as we realize that our words matter and that they have the power to influence our daily lives. Being confident in your unique expressions is a key stepping stone to growing as an individual and allows us to validate, appreciate, and believe in our thoughts. It guides us to stand up for our beliefs, pursue our dreams, build relationships, find our identity, and reinforce our self-assurance (Back on Track Teens, 2021).

THE ART OF CONVERSATION STARTING

Striking up a conversation is a universal challenge for most people, whether it be giving a major presentation or engaging in idle chit-chat, but don't sweat it; these tips will help you start up a conversation with anybody:

Tip One: Cliche's and Small Talk Are a No-No

"How's the weather?" or "How about that traffic, right?" isn't any better than a cringy pick-up line, so avoid them at all costs; they can make a conversation dry up instantly, and the situation can quickly turn awkward.

Tip Two: Seek Opinions

Instead of tired topics, seek opinions. Start with light topics like music, food, or the atmosphere you're in. For instance, "What did you think of Drake's new album?" These questions open up more room for discussion than a quick one-word answer.

Tip Three: Ask for Recommendations

Asking for recommendations is a great icebreaker; it shows you value their opinion and allows them to set the pace of the conversation. For instance, "I just finished Wednesday; I need something else to watch on Netflix. Any ideas?"

Tip Four: Find Common Interests

People enjoy discussing their interests, whether it's their hobbies, their favorite sports team, pets, or favorite video game. People are more likely to open up when talking about something they are passionate about.

Tip Five: Request Updates or Further Explanation

Asking for updates from your classmates is a great way to break the ice and naturally start a conversation. Ask them what the homework for science class is or if they know anything more about the class field trip coming up. This may seem simple, but it can evolve into a genuine conversation.

Tip Six: Avoid Asking One-Word Reply Questions

Ask open-ended questions that invite detailed responses instead of dreaded "yes" or "no" answers. Be proactive and prepare follow-up questions to guide the flow of conversation and deepen engagement. Instead of asking, "How was your weekend?" ask, "How was your weekend? Did you get up to anything interesting?" This helps open the conversation a little further and avoids the chance of being told just "yes" or "no" (Marr, 2014).

PUBLIC SPEAKING TIPS FOR TEENS

If you get anxious when it comes to public speaking, you're not alone; public speaking is often right near the top of any teenage anxiety list. Consider these tips to improve your confidence when addressing a crowd:

Tip One: Believe In What You Are Saying

If you don't believe what you are saying, how can you expect anybody else to either? If you want to get through to others, influence them, and capture their attention, self-belief is a non-negotiable.

Tip Two: Simplicity Over Complexity

Contrary to popular belief, using sophisticated and convoluted language doesn't make your delivery more impressive; in most cases, it does the opposite. It leads to misunderstandings and perceptions of being overly smart. A clear and concise message is the key to truly connecting with others. Understanding that simplicity is better received helps to ease the fear of failure.

Tip Three: Be Mindful of Your Body Language and Wardrobe

How we communicate with non-verbal cues and how we dress is a game changer and creates the illusion of confidence in addressing an audience, even if we, don't feel all that confident. How we present ourselves sets the tone for all that follows. Poor posture indicates a lack of confidence and detracts from the message while making eye contact, adopting an assertive tone, and opening up our bodies to the crowd inspire engagement from the audience.

Tip Four: Pause and Move On

If you mess up the pronunciation of a word, don't panic; if you skipped a line on your cue card, don't panic; if you delivered a joke and nobody got it, don't panic. The bottom line, panicking will never help; don't harp on a mistake we all make. Take a quick pause, take a breath to compose yourself, and move on.

Tip Five: Be Kind to Yourself

Not receiving a standing ovation doesn't define a successful speech, getting one is the cherry on top, but it shouldn't be your reason to do something. After your speech, give yourself credit. Speaking in public is an achievement many fear worldwide, and you conquered it. Be kind to yourself. (The Big Red Group, 2022).

HOW TO EXPRESS YOUR NEEDS AND OPINIONS RESPECTFULLY

To effectively express our needs and opinions to others respectfully, we need to adopt an assertive approach to communication. What this ultimately means is that we need to express our needs and opinions respectfully through honest and open dialogue. Assertiveness is not the same as aggression. When we are assertive in our approach to communication, we acknowledge how others feel while still standing firm in our stance about our values, beliefs, needs, and opinions, thus promoting a balanced exchange of perspectives respectfully.

There are several ways we can enhance our assertive communication skills:

- Consider all perspectives and refrain from judgment or exaggeration
- Using "I" statements, such as "I feel like you aren't listening when I try to express myself.". This approach emphasizes our needs and opinions without placing blame on the other person.
- List behavior, results, and feelings; for instance, "When you talk over me, I can't get my point across, and I feel ignored."
- Focusing on body language helps us understand how others are reacting and also plays a role in how others receive our

message. Stand tall, sustain eye contact, and stay composed. Employ a firm yet friendly tone.

- Put it all together by using this formula: "When you [their behavior], I feel [your feelings]." For instance, "When you ignore my point of view, I feel like you don't care what I have to say."

It may take time to master assertive communication, but its benefits are invaluable. It helps us to establish boundaries, amplify our voices so our needs are considered, and cultivate mutual respect. (Scott, 2019).

ROLE-PLAYING SCENARIOS TO PRACTICE SPEAKING WITH CONFIDENCE.

It's practice time. Mastering confident communication can take time, so the more we practice, the better we'll get at it. Make use of these role-playing scenarios with a small group to cultivate confidence, tackle conflict, and enhance effective communication.

Scenario One: Plans for the Weekend

It's the weekend, and you and your buddies are deciding how you want to spend it. Some friends want to go see a movie; others want to go hang out on the beach. It's up to you to confidently express your preference, consider both your desires and the group's other desires, and come up with a compromise or get everybody on board with your idea.

Scenario Two: Shakespeare Skit

You have a group assignment for English to put on a Shakespearean skit, however, some of your group members are not participating and slowing down the process. Address this issue confidently by taking the lead, expressing your concerns, and suggesting a collaborative solution where everyone is involved and actively participating.

While communication is a key component of our journey of self-confidence, so is understanding the impact of our digital lives.

NAVIGATING THE DIGITAL WORLD CONFIDENTLY

Technology is a wonderful gift that offers many benefits and conveniences. However, when we misuse our devices and become overly dependent on them, they can have profoundly negative effects on our self-perception, self-belief, and self-worth, underscoring the importance of using technology mindfully and responsibly.

A recent study found that the average teenager spends 8 hours and 39 minutes a day glued to their device's screens. That's one-third of the day. Another third of the day is dedicated to sleep, which ultimately means teenagers are left with approximately one-third to engage in school work, socializing, and attending to various other responsibilities.

If we take these numbers further, we can determine that the average teenager's screen time over a week is slightly over 60 hours. This translates to approximately two and a half days of screen time every week, totaling 130 days a year (My Kids Vision, 2022).

Evaluating these numbers reveals that we need to reassess our reliance on our digital devices, and the need for change is all too apparent.

THE IMPACT OF SOCIAL MEDIA ON CONFIDENCE

Social comparisons are not new; they are an age-old tendency, a habit humans have used since the dawn of time to gauge their progress relative to others. Social comparisons are not necessarily harmful; if used correctly, they serve as inspiration and motivation that help us pursue our passions or seek meaningful relationships. The problem is that when social media use became widespread, it amplified our natural inclination to compare ourselves.

Social media is focused on curated online content, highlighting our successes and ignoring our failures, creating the illusion of perfection. Therefore, comparing ourselves online with others is not a benchmark for the full picture. Additionally, we have more access to compare ourselves with others than ever. Constantly comparing ourselves is detrimental. In essence, social media amplifies opportunities for comparison and feelings of inadequacy.

Constant exposure to glorified posts ensnares us in a cycle of self-comparison and hurts our psyche. It diminishes our positive mood, leading to an environment of envy and discontent (Ries, 2022).

I used to have a complicated relationship with social media. Don't get me wrong, I love social media. It's a fantastic platform to build new connections, reconnect with old friends, engage in amazing content, and inform us on many topics. However, I am also acutely aware of the dangers it possesses. I used to find myself mindfully scrolling on social media platforms for countless hours, and while it gave me rushes of dopamine at the time, I gradually accumulated the detrimental impacts of these platforms as time progressed. In those moments of aimless scrolling, I began to subconsciously compare myself against the curated narratives of others. Their achievements, their stunning relationships, and their seemingly flawless lives.

I didn't realize it at the time, but I started noticing my self-confidence taking a nosedive. I began to see myself in a less favorable light, and as the persistent comparisons continued, my sense of self-worth drastically declined. I realized something needed to change, so I decided to use these platforms more mindfully.

STRATEGIES TO USE SOCIAL MEDIA MINDFULLY

My goal was not to stop using social media altogether; rather, I needed to change how I was using it so I could regain control over my thoughts and reclaim the self-worth that I had lost.

Strategy One: Recognize the Illusion of Social Media

Keep in mind that most social media posts represent a carefully curated and idealized version of their lives, showing us the highlights reel but not the struggles along the way. You may see your friends holidaying in Greece, and everything looks wonderful, but you never saw any of the challenges behind that post.

Strategy Two: Monitor and Track Your Social Media Habits

Monitor how much time you spend on social media, and track the moments you find yourself comparing your life to others. Try to look for and understand usage patterns (time of day, place, types of posts you view, etc.) and your emotions when scrolling. Based on your findings, adjust your behavior. Consider turning off your notifications or avoiding scrolling at specific times to reduce feelings of negativity.

Strategy Three: Be Selective With Your Online Circle

If specific individuals or accounts consistently make you feel bad about yourself or trigger negative thoughts through their posts, cut them out and unfollow them. Be deliberate with whom you follow based on their positive impact on your life.

Strategy Four: Nurture Real-Life Relationships

We shouldn't take our offline relationships for granted. We must recognize that physical interactions offer more context and positivity than online comparisons. Don't judge people based on what they post as fact; rather, engage in conversations to understand the full picture. By surrounding ourselves with trusted offline relationships, we can balance out the negative effects of online comparisons.

Strategy Five: Engage In A Digital Detox Every Now and Then

Don't be afraid to disengage from social media completely. Personally, there is nothing more liberating than engaging in a temporary digital detox. When I find myself stuck in a loop of online comparisons, I uninstall my social media app. It's liberating. It helps me clear my mind, focus on myself, diminish the temptation to scroll, and ignore the need to compare myself to others.

A digital detox doesn't necessarily have to be a long-term commitment. Research indicates that simply taking a one-week hiatus from social media enhances our mental health and helps break the addictive cycle of scrolling and comparing.

Social media's impact on the brain's reward center through injecting small doses of dopamine makes it potentially habit-forming, leading to increased usage, even if we are aware of its harmful effects. Stepping back and deleting these apps serves as a reality check and helps us recognize how reliant we are on these platforms. A digital detox gives us time to self-reflect and refrain from engaging in toxic activities that hinder our growth. Personally, distancing myself helps put perceived shortcomings into perspective, realizing that others' flawless posts don't define my success (Ries, 2022).

CYBERBULLYING AND ONLINE HARASSMENT

With the introduction of technology came a new wave of bullying. This wave is known as cyberbullying and has become a looming dark cloud for countless teens over the past few decades. Research shows that 37% of individuals aged 12 to 17 have experienced cyberbullying one way or another, while 30% have experienced it on multiple occasions (Do Something, 2019).

Cyberbullying is when somebody uses technology to harass, threaten, or humiliate others. It can take on many forms, including racism, sharing hurtful photos, blackmail through personal information, sexism, stalking, overtly nasty messages, and any other forms of bullying tactics in an online setting. Cyberbullying is just as harmful, if not more harmful, than regular bullying and can lead to serious distress in victims. It can influence low self-esteem, anxiety, depression, and suicidal thoughts. Its effects are incredibly pervasive, shattering the victim's self-worth and self-confidence, causing a disconnect with reality, and severely impacting the victim's overall well-being, both physically and mentally.

There are many signs to watch out for to help recognize if somebody is being targeted through cyberbullying tactics. Victims will:

- Demonstrate emotional distress during and after digital activity.
- Adopt increased secrecy about their digital life.
- Spend excessive time on their own.

- Withdraw from relationships with their friends, family, and other important people in their lives.
- Their academic performance will decline.
- They will showcase depressive symptoms and withdraw from situations that once brought them joy.
- They Have significant changes in their mood, behavior, sleep patterns, and appetite (Nemours Kids Health, 2024).

Due to the rising prevalence of cyberbullying and its disastrous consequences, there is an urgent need for awareness, prevention, and support mechanisms to safeguard our overall well-being against bullying tactics in the digital age.

HOW TO RESPOND TO ONLINE HARASSMENT

Cyberbullying can be extremely intense, leaving us feeling emotionally and mentally overwhelmed and significantly impacting our overall quality of life. We feel trapped and want it to stop, but we don't always know how. Dealing with a cyberbully can be challenging, but there are ways we can deal with it and protect ourselves from online harassment. Follow these tips to handle online harassment effectively:

Tip One: Do Not Respond Immediately

This is easier said than done, as our natural reaction would be to defend ourselves by fighting back. However, don't give them that satisfaction. Not only do they want to elicit a response from us, but responding can exacerbate the situation. The best course of action is to put your device down and take a step back.

Tip Two: Block the Sender

If harassment continues after you have ignored them, the best thing you can do is to block that contact. This helps us take back control of our online environment. If the cyberbully continues to contact you on multiple phone numbers, keep blocking them.

Tip Three: Keep the Message

Even if you have blocked the contact, keep the message they sent, no matter how hurtful or painful it may be. You don't even have to read it, but keep it as proof, so if you need to seek help from others, you have evidence. Many websites, mobile phone companies, and law enforcement require proof before taking action. Empower yourself by reporting offensive content to relevant platforms so they can help you deal with your situation.

Tip Four: Seek Support

Confide in your support system. Share your experience with an authority figure and those you trust dearly to seek guidance. If the cyberbullying intensifies and becomes severe, don't be afraid to involve the police or other relevant organizations that can ensure your safety.

This helps foster safety and emotional strength, enhance our resistance to the situation, give us a sense of belonging, and take back the cyberbully's control (Webwise, 2019).

Tip Five: Remember, It's Not Your Fault

Never blame yourself; any act of cyberbullying is not your fault. You cannot control how others act; you are the victim here, not the cause of the issue.

Blocking and reporting a contact, in conjunction with saving any evidence of cyberbullying, is the most important step we can take to end cyberbullying onslaughts.

SUPPORTING FRIENDS FACING CYBERBULLYING

Just as we would need support if we experienced cyberbullying, our friends need help, too. We can support our friends in their time of need by reassuring them of their bravery and encouraging them to engage in open and honest conversations about what is going on.

We can also help collect evidence of cyberbullying behavior by urging them to take screenshots of messages and advising them to block and report their cyberbullying. We can review the privacy settings on their devices for added security and accompany them as a pillar of support when they approach an authority figure, their parents, school counselors, teachers, or anyone they trust who can help with their situation. Additionally, we can encourage them to see a therapist to work through the negative emotions they are feeling as a result of cyberbullying attacks.

While we can't necessarily fix the problem, we can be empathetic and provide support to help make a meaningful difference as our friends navigate through cyberbullying challenges.

CREATING A POSITIVE DIGITAL FOOTPRINT

Our digital footprint is like a trail of breadcrumbs that the world can keep track of. Whenever we engage in online activities such as posting on social media, browsing the web, chatting online, or even shopping, we leave a trail for the world to follow and get a sense of who we are.

If we disregard the significant impact our digital footprint has on our future endeavors, relationships, and reputation, we will be making a grave error. Remember that our digital footprint consists of the content we willingly share as well as invisible components that can be tracked through our IP address and browser history. Therefore, our digital footprint consists of online actions that we may not consider immediately apparent, making it even more imperative to be mindful of the digital traces, especially on social media.

Make use of these tips to cultivate a meaningful and positive digital footprint:

- Refrain from sharing too much personal information, especially on social media
- Utilize thoughtful posting (consider how your comments, photos, or videos might be perceived by others before posting).
- Implement privacy settings on your accounts.
- Do not share content or comment on other posts impulsively or based on negative emotions such as stress or anger. Instead, step back and give yourself time to cool off before engaging with a post.
- Monitor the online accounts you do use, and consider deleting any accounts that may lead to a tainted reputation offline.

- Search yourself on Google and see how search engines view your profile to understand how other searches will perceive you.
- Make sure the passwords for your accounts are strong and unique for each platform.
- Review the security settings on your devices and install a security solution to help protect against any phishing attempts or malicious hacking (Bizga, 2022)

Always remember that we control the information we wish to share online. Thus, we need to focus on creating a digital footprint comprising a positive narrative that will not be easily misinterpreted or used against us to harm our reputation offline.

If done correctly, we will formulate a strong and positive online reputation with numerous benefits, including:

- It's a window into our passions, aspirations, interests, and hobbies so others can see what we stand for and what we like. If these are positive, it will foster a favorable reputation for those who don't know us well.
- It builds trust and credibility among our peers and online communities through various positive interactions online.
- It highlights our creativity and gives extra context to our personalities, so we can stand out in the vast digital landscape.
- Showcases our skills, talents, and qualifications, boosting prospects for employment and connections with others.
- Encourages constructive and authentic engagements with others online, resulting in more meaningful interactions and connections.
- A positive digital identity can influence and inspire others through a ripple effect that encourages constructive

behavior and a supportive online environment.

JOIN ONLINE COMMUNITIES, SHARE YOUR PASSIONS, AND CELEBRATE YOUR ACHIEVEMENTS

Don't mistake this for a means of bragging, but rather your way to tell the world, "Here I am; this is me." A little humble display can spread joy, inspiration, and motivation to others while showcasing who we are as people. It is a crucial element in building a positive digital identity.

Sharing our passions and achievements helps us find our unique voice online. This voice is authentically who we are and will resonate with others, inspiring them to explore their passions through the influence of our enthusiasm. Humans are attracted to authentic behavior and passion.

Connecting with like-minded individuals or online communities that share our interests helps amplify our joy, expand our knowledge, and foster comradery through a common passion. When we share our passion and achievements, we help guide others on their passionate journeys. Using social media or setting up a personal blog are fantastic ways to showcase your interests, inspire others, and build relationships with a wide range of people.

Collaborating with others is another avenue many take to enhance their passions further. When we join forces with like-minded communities, we forge meaningful relationships, empowering us to collectively employ initiatives that foster growth, for ourselves and others. This collaboration promotes shared interests and allows us to celebrate mutual achievements. In essence, sharing what lights our fire and showcasing our achievements is not meant to make us feel superior; it is meant to enhance our online identity and inspire those around us to grow as individuals (DK, 2023).

EVERLEIGH ROSE, THE INFLUENCER WHO RADIATES POSITIVITY WITH A LARGER-THAN-LIFE PRESENCE AT JUST 12 YEARS OLD

At just 12 years old, influencer Everleigh Rose has become a prominent figure on social media. Her channel presents diverse inspiring content, such as dance routines, vlogs, family escapades, and engaging "get-ready-with-me" videos.

Her content serves as a wellspring of inspiration that motivates people to live life to the fullest through her positivity and zest for life. Her channel is a prime example of having a positive digital identity, giving her followers a glimpse into her dynamic and uplifting personality. Whether she's showcasing her creativity through dance or putting smiles on the faces of millions of her followers, she leaves her viewers with a sense of joy for life's simple pleasures and beautiful moments waiting to be shared with those we love (GRIN, 2018).

While the digital world provides us with opportunities to be mindful of how we present ourselves, we also need to cultivate resilience for real-life challenges.

MAKE A DIFFERENCE WITH YOUR WORDS

Spread the Joy of Confidence

"Self-confidence is like a magic key that opens the door to new possibilities."

— UNKNOWN

Did you know that people who share kindness and support often find themselves swimming in a sea of happiness and success? Well, it's true, and if there's a chance to spread that joy here, you bet we're going to take it!

Here's a little question for you...

Would you lend a hand to someone you've never met, even if you knew your name wouldn't be remembered for it?

Now, who might this person be? They're a bit like you once were. Maybe a little unsure of themselves, eager to make a mark in the world but not quite sure how or where to start seeking guidance.

Our goal is to ensure Self-confidence For Teens finds its way into the hands and hearts of every teen. Everything WE do is driven by this goal. And the only way to truly achieve this is to reach... well, every single teen out there.

I'm reaching out on behalf of those teens you've never met:

Could you please support a teen in finding their confidence by writing a review for this book?

It's a simple act that doesn't cost a dime and takes less than a minute, but it has the potential to profoundly impact a Teen who is just starting their journey towards self-belief. Your review might be the nudge they need to...

...feel more connected and supported in their community. ...take that first brave step towards their dreams. ...find meaningful ways to express themselves. ...discover strategies to overcome their challenges. ...see a dream of theirs come to life.

To experience that wonderful feeling of making a difference, all you need to do is... take less than 60 seconds to... write a review.

Just scan the QR code below to leave your review:

If the thought of helping a teen learn to navigate social challenges warms your heart, then you're definitely my kind of person. Welcome to the club. You're one of the good ones.

I'm even more excited to help you build your confidence, improve your mental health, and become a social butterfly quicker and more smoothly than you ever thought possible. You're going to find the activities, strategies, and tips in the upcoming chapters incredibly helpful.

Thank you from the deepest part of my heart. Now, let's get back to boosting that confidence.

- Your biggest cheerleader, Aubrey Andrus

PS - Fun fact: Sharing something valuable with someone else not only helps them but also increases your value in their eyes. If you want to spread a little joy among teens and you believe this book can make a difference, why not share it with someone who could use it?

BUILDING RESILIENCE

THE COMPONENTS OF RESILIENCE

Resilience is commonly believed to be the iron will we summon when adversity strikes so that we can bounce back on our feet. While this is correct, it represents just a single element of resilience, and although it may be the most crucial aspect, resilience encompasses a broader range of attributes and factors. We must remember that if we simply react impulsively to *bounce back*, we may find ourselves marching head-first in an undesired direction. If we view resilience from a somatic understanding, "it is our capacity to holistically return to center (Connolly, 2020)."

This means resilience involves connecting with our body, thoughts, emotions, and reactions without judgment. Through connecting these pieces, we can undergo a deliberate process of assessing, acknowledging, and choosing a plan of action to overcome a challenge. Through this process, we can cultivate a new state and return to the challenges we face with greater purpose, broader perspectives, and new creative solutions.

Building resilience is like strengthening a muscle; it requires effort to enhance our self-awareness, self-care, and flexibility and form broader perspectives.

Component One: Self-Awareness

Recognizing, acknowledging, and understanding our emotions without judgment can provide a grounded response to tackle adversity effectively. Additionally, understanding and accepting both our strengths and weaknesses enables a balanced and adaptable mindset when tackling a problem.

Component Two: Self-Care

If we don't care for ourselves, we won't be able to face challenges effectively. Regular exercise, a healthy diet, and sufficient rest are essential to facing challenges with the energy and resilience needed to overcome them. We maintain and improve our mental and emotional well-being through relaxation and joyful activities to become more resilient when faced with challenges.

Component Three: Flexibility

Adopting a mindset that embraces change and can easily adapt to evolving circumstances allows us to face challenges with more resourceful approaches. Reframing setbacks into opportunities, and encouraging positive thinking helps develop an optimistic and resilient outlook on life.

Component Four: Looking at the Bigger Picture

When we align our short-term goals with our long-term objectives, we prevent temporary setbacks and foster steady progress toward overcoming obstacles. Remember, no man is an island, and finding comfort and support from our support system will not only console us when times are tough but also provide diverse perspectives for collaborative problem-solving (Connolly, 2020).

THE ROLE OF MINDSET IN RESILIENCE

Mindset truly determines resilience. A resilient mindset keeps our fire burning and pushes us to become better versions of ourselves. It enables us to embrace challenges, persist through setbacks, and seek guidance from others. Adopting a resilient mindset allows us to see failures as opportunities to improve and bounce back even stronger than when we began.

It takes time to cultivate a mindset as resilient as this, but through these tips, we will be able to strengthen our minds and spirits to overcome any obstacle in our way:

Tip One: Find Daily Meaning

Make every day matter. Incorporate activities and goals that inject a sense of success and purpose daily. This gives us direction, motivation, and inspiration to take on each day with vigor and high spirits.

Tip Two: Strengthen Your Relationship With Those You Love and Respect

These relationships are crucial throughout our lives, through good and challenging times; they bring joy and color to our worlds and help us grow as individuals emotionally and mentally. Our relationships inspire, motivate, and drive us to be our best.

Tip Three: Reflect on How You Handled Challenges in the Past

Think back to how you handled challenges in the past. Reflect on what coping strategies worked and which ones didn't. Reevaluating the past can help us identify patterns we can adopt and learn from our mistakes to guide our desirable behavior and perspectives in the future.

Tip Four: Maintaining Hope

No matter how bleak a situation may seem, it is never hopeless. While we can't change the past, we can learn from it, and with those lessons, we can adopt new behaviors and coping mechanisms to deal with future challenges. Staying hopeful is key to a resilient mindset.

Tip Five: Embrace A Growth Mindset

A growth mindset goes hand in hand with a resilient mindset. Embracing a growth mindset means acknowledging the limitless potential for learning and growth. We believe in our strengths, understand our weaknesses, and adapt to setbacks by viewing them as opportunities to grow and broaden our capabilities and perspectives (Mayo Clinic, 2020b).

OVERCOMING CHALLENGES THROUGH RESILIENCE MAKES US STRONGER

When we are resilient, we shake off the obstacles holding us back despite the odds and confidently look forward to finding ways to grow. When we overcome our problems through resilience and perseverance, we build strength and elevate our mindset to one that can endure and thrive in the face of adversity.

As we build on our resilience, we become more capable of navigating challenging situations and demonstrating our ability to tackle challenges with creativity, innovation, and effectiveness. We clear our minds from worry and panic to stay focused on our goals and grow stronger with each obstacle we overcome.

We become more adaptable and flexible. We change our mindset, freeing our minds from negativity, and adopt new ways to overcome our problems based on changing circumstances. Recovering from unpleasant situations requires effort and time, but resilient individuals do not let challenges distract them from growing and learning from setbacks (People Builders, 2022).

COPING STRATEGIES FOR TOUGH TIMES

Life is stressful; we face many challenges, and some days are especially tough. Being faced with all these challenges is hard enough, but trying to control every single aspect at play will only bring us down, make us frustrated, and exacerbate an already challenging situation into an even harder one to deal with. To lighten the load, we must remember that only certain things are within our control. The four most important aspects are our attitude, behavior, values, and purpose.

Teenagers often get caught up in the idea that they lack control over situations, given the extensive external factors that influence their lives. The rapid changes they undergo, the social desire to fit in, expectations from others, or various other factors leave them feeling overwhelmed. Nevertheless, we must remember that we are not defined by what happens to us but by how we respond to those experiences. The key is that as long as we focus on controlling what is in our control, coping with difficult challenges will become far more manageable. This is because we will only be accountable for what we can do, not what others do. The power lies in our choices, not what external factors come into play (True Sport, 2023).

Understanding what we can and can't control will greatly influence how we view and face challenges in the future. Consider what we can and can't control:

Can Control	Can't Control
Our attitude/mindset	Other people's expectations of us
Our values	How people treat us and their actions
Our beliefs	Our past
Our purpose	Change
Our behaviors	Genetics
How we structure our day	World events
How we treat others	Our age
How we respond to negativity?	Injustice and unfairness placed upon us by others
How do we care for our mental health?	Accidents

(Christian, 2021)

FINDING AND BUILDING YOUR SUPPORT NETWORK

The strength of resilient individuals frequently lies in their robust network of supportive relationships. Finding and building a dependable support network helps us overcome difficult times. Within these invaluable connections, individuals find emotional support, practical guidance, and a profound sense of belonging, which are essential for our overall emotional and mental well-being.

According to Maslow's hierarchy of needs, a sense of belonging (our support system) ranks third in importance among all our needs. Only physiological (food, warmth, etc.) and safety (security and absence of immediate danger) rank higher (Suicide Call Back Service, 2023).

Finding and building a robust support system cannot be understated when highlighting its role in our overall well-being. We can find support from our family, friends, classmates, neighbors, acquaintances, online communities, and local communities.

Family

Through open communication, active listening, and spending quality time with our family, we can build trust and mutual understanding, cultivating healthy relationships with our family members and building a strong foundation of support.

Friends

Friends are a crucial piece of this puzzle. Unlike family, our friends are chosen, making it crucial to select them wisely. Seek empathetic friends who uplift, support, and guide you, as well as friends who share common interests and values, ultimately bringing joy into your life. Friends offer us unique perspectives and provide external support.

Classmates and Teachers

These relationships support us on our journey to achieving our educational goals. Forge connections with classmates who share similar interests and who are striving for similar goals. Look for mentorship opportunities from a teacher or somebody you respect to provide you with support to grow as a scholar and individual.

Neighbors and Acquaintances

Expand your network by reaching out to those in your existing circle and attending community events to meet new people who share your interests.

Online Communities

Join online communities aligned with your interests and values to find support and connect with like-minded individuals on social media.

Local Communities

Interact with your local community by joining a sports team, volunteering, or attending social events in your area. This type of support helps create a sense of belonging and purpose.

Remember that individuals in our network may provide diverse forms of support, highlighting the value of having a broad range of connections for friendship, parental guidance, mentorship, and assistance. Having a robust and reliable support system will make a world of difference when processing and coping with challenging times (Suicide Call Back Service, 2023).

FINDING HEALTHY OUTLETS FOR EMOTIONS

Bad days happen, but how we work through our emotions when those days come is what makes us more resilient. Personally, I find solace in writing. It provides a safe outlet for expressing and processing emotions, allowing me to be more rational by giving me time to contemplate my feelings before conveying them verbally.

At the end of the day, that's my positive outlet for managing my emotions on a tough day, but there are loads of other ways to do it such as:

Regular Exercise

Hit the gym. I'm sure you've been told countless times that exercise is good for you, which it is! But it's not only good to help strengthen your muscles and boost cardiovascular health; it's a fantastic way to improve your mood, too. Whether you decide to run, walk, dance, do yoga, play basketball or throw the old pig skin around, it's an incredibly effective way to work through your emotions constructively and positively.

Writing

If you are like me, you can try writing. It's a wonderful way to create distance from whatever's troubling. It helps us tackle problems with a clearer perspective guided by rational thinking instead of reacting emotionally. Plus, it's a great way to lighten our emotional load when we put our troubles on paper!

Talking it Out With Someone You Trust

Sometimes, talking is the best medicine. If we struggle to work through challenging emotions on our own, we can always confide in our support system for advice, or just having an ear to bend can be incredibly effective.

Verbalizing our emotions helps to unburden our hearts and minds. Expressing emotions verbally can offer insights into our perspectives and even provide a broader lens for overcoming challenges through others' perspectives we never considered.

Crying Can Be Beneficial, Not a Weaknesses

Crying is neither gender or age-assigned behavior; anybody can cry, and don't let anyone tell you otherwise. Crying helps accelerate healing. Letting go of our emotions through crying, or even screaming and yelling, in a safe space, in conjunction with positively reframing our emotions, can do the world of good.

Deep Breathing

Deep breathing is extremely effective for grounding ourselves and helps us reclaim a sense of calm during moments of panic and anxiety. It helps us shift our perspective from acting emotionally to acting rationally, thus clearing our minds and reducing the feeling of an imminent threat. Refer back to Chapter 3 to practice breathing techniques.

Practice Forgiveness

While forgiveness isn't necessarily an outlet, it is essential to overcome many challenges or burdens holding us back. To move on and heal from the pain caused by others or the guilt we inflict upon ourselves, we need to learn to forgive. Forgiving isn't easy, but through forgiveness, we can let go of feelings of anger, revenge, or resentment that stop us from growing. It isn't hurting anybody else but ourselves (Positivity Guides, 2022).

OVERCOMING RESILIENCE TO BECOME A GLOBAL ICON

Michael Jordan, the global basketball idol, didn't just become the global and beloved superstar he is today without working relentlessly towards his goal and being fiercely resilient to overcome any obstacle that was in his way.

Arguably, his biggest obstacle was his time as a high school basketball player. Believe it or not, he was cut from his high school team for reasons that are hard to imagine, knowing what he would go on to achieve. He was cut because his coaches believed he lacked the talent, the drive, and the height necessary to make it, not even as a pro, but as a starting high school player. Now, Michael could have easily given way back then. He could have told himself, "Well, he's the coach; he must know what he's talking about," but he didn't, and thank goodness he didn't, because he would never have reached the monumental heights he went on to achieve.

Instead of being down on himself, Michael transformed that setback into motivation. Determined to prove to himself and others that he was star material, he worked tirelessly and transcended expectations, reshaping the sport, leaving an indelible mark as an iconic athlete, and inspiring millions. His journey from rejection to unparalleled success stands as a testament to resilience, drive, and the ability to turn adversity into triumph (Johal, 2020).

BOUNCING BACK FROM FAILURE

If there's one thing I know, it's that we need to embrace failure and redefine the concept of what failing means. Winston Churchill once said, "Success is not final, and failure is not fatal; it is the courage to continue that counts." This is a fantastic way to view failure; it demonstrates that failure should be viewed as a powerful tool to learn and progress, that fosters creativity, and opens us up to new experiences.

Think about a sports team. They practice tirelessly throughout the week before a game. Of course, it is to hone their skills, but it could also be seen as the willingness to accumulate a variety of well-calibrated mistakes to learn from and improve upon.

The fear of failure is not something we are born with; it is something we pick up as we grow older. Think of young children around four or five years old; they exhibit no fear of failure; they try new things, stumble, fail, get back up, and learn rapidly from their repeated "failures."

So, the key here is to redefine what failure means to us. Our focus should be on failing forward and mastering the art of failing. Essentially, we need to take risks, learn from our experiences when we don't succeed, resist the urge to blame ourselves or others, and avoid the tendency to completely ignore failure so that we can effectively handle failure in the future (Syed, 2015).

LEARNING FROM OUR MISTAKES

While failure and mistakes may seem the same on the surface, there is a slight difference. A failure is often the result of an incorrect action, while a mistake is typically the incorrect action itself. When we make mistakes, there is an opportunity to learn and rectify what we did wrong, however, with failure, learning is typically the only outcome. That being said, how do we learn from and rectify our mistakes (MasterClass, 2022)?

Step One: Acknowledge and Admit Your Mistakes

The learning process can only begin once we accept and admit we have made an error. It's important to apologize if our mistakes have impacted others. Apologizing not only demonstrates honesty and responsibility but also shows our commitment to making improvements. Furthermore, apologizing relieves the burden of carrying our mistakes alone.

Step Two: Reframe Mistakes as Lessons

Embrace mistakes as opportunities for learning and growth, fostering a mindset focused on improvement. Let go of any feelings of embarrassment or shame and recognize that we all make mistakes. When we view mistakes as lessons, we naturally avoid hiding from them or distributing blame.

Step Three: Analyze Your Mistake

Try to understand the cause behind your mistake. Reflect on your intentions, what went wrong, why it happened, and how to prevent it from happening again. This will empower us to make different choices should the same or a similar situation repeat itself.

Step Four: Set Realistic and Achievable Goals for Yourself

Keeping our goals and expectations realistic helps guide us along our improvement journey. It's important to shoot for the stars; just make sure they are within our grasp and that we are not putting unnecessary pressure on ourselves to learn from our mistakes if it is out of our control to rectify them. Instead, aim for steady progress, with actionable steps to help us grow.

Step Five: Implement the Lessons You Learned

Apply what you've learned, adapt based on the knowledge you've acquired, improve your communication style, break or form new habits, and put any other necessary rectifying actions into motion. We can grow and thrive as individuals when we embrace the complexity of experiencing something new, accept our imperfections, and realize that mistakes are part of the learning process.

Step Six: Track Your Progress and Cultivate a Growth Mindset

Just take a minute to see how far you've come and monitor how much you have grown from learning from your past mistakes. This helps boost our self-confidence and enables us to take pride in our strides. Identify what works for you and what areas you still need to improve upon. Always work on developing a strong growth mindset, as this is essential to avoid the pitfalls of perfectionism and helps us maintain focus for continuous learning and improvement (MasterClass, 2022).

Step Seven: Be Persistent and Celebrate Progress, Not Just Success

We need to keep at it and recognize that improving ourselves is an ongoing journey. Learning from our mistakes is not always a quick fix, and it often takes time. Don't be disheartened if your progress isn't going as quickly as you'd like. Keep persisting, and remember that slow and steady wins the race. We need to understand that success doesn't come overnight; it is the result of persistent hard work and steady progress. Celebrate any progress you make, no matter how big or small; that incremental growth drives us to keep marching forward.

While resilience may help us bounce back on our feet, setting and achieving goals helps propel us forward!

GOAL SETTING AND ACHIEVEMENT

According to research by Dominican University, people who establish goals for themselves are 43 percent more likely to attain them successfully. What's more, the same study found that individuals who set specific and challenging goals for themselves were even more likely to achieve success compared to individuals who set easier goals for themselves (Shahid, 2023).

UNDERSTANDING OUR VALUES AND INTERESTS

What matters most to you? Only we can answer that as individuals. It requires digging deep and reflecting on what makes us who we are. Often, we can identify what matters most to us by identifying aspects of our lives that bring us happiness and fulfillment, or it could be an aspiration we tirelessly pursue.

Sometimes, going down memory lane and reflecting on moments, hobbies, or people from our past that once ignited a passion in our hearts helps us identify what truly matters to us most. Reassessing these neglected aspects could reignite a spark within us. We can also identify what matters most to us by seeking what we deem irreplaceable or something we cannot live without. Whether it be a dream, our family, our friends, an interest that lights a fire in us, our values, or a combination of them all, understanding what matters most to us deepens our understanding of ourselves, what we can't live without, and our goals in life (Morning Coach, 2022).

SETTING GOALS THAT ALIGN WITH OUR INTERESTS AND VALUES

Goals should reflect who we are; they should be embedded in our identity. Your goals should align with your passions and values. When our goals resonate with our interests and passions, we are more likely to stay motivated and committed as we pursue them. When our goals align with our values, we'll experience greater satisfaction when we achieve them, as they will be in harmony with our core beliefs and principles (Eatough, 2021).

People often neglect that setting meaningful goals goes beyond simply achieving external success; it's a journey of personal growth and fulfillment. As we undergo this journey, we should feel a sense of pride and accomplishment once we achieve our goals. Aligning our interests and values with our goals helps guide us toward a life that is more meaningful and fulfilling to us (Sheanoy, 2023).

In high school, we often fall into the trap of setting our goals based on what we feel others want from us. I was no different; in my senior year at high school, I was pursuing goals that I believed others wanted me to achieve, but I found I had no motivation or drive to make them a reality, nor did I take much satisfaction when I made progress towards them. That's when I stepped back and looked deep within myself. I realized these goals weren't my own and didn't align with who I was.

Through self-discovery and asking the question, "Who am I?" I discovered that I wanted to help people become the most confident version of themselves. Once I realized I had reevaluated my goals, I had far more motivation. I felt good about myself for achieving the steps needed to reach this goal, and today, I have helped countless people realize their potential.

EXERCISE: UNCOVERING YOUR VALUES

This exercise aims to help you self-reflect and gain personal insights about your values. Follow the exercise in chronological order below:

Step 1: List Values

Write down what matters most to you on sticky notes. Focus on values, not tangible things such as people or material possessions; use abstract concepts such as "compassion" or "integrity." Give yourself 5 minutes to write down as many as you think apply to you.

Step 2: Reflect on Positive Experiences in the Past

Recall past events, memories, and fulfilling emotions. Identify why those memories brought or still bring you joy. Reflect on proud moments and highlight what fulfillment and happiness mean to you.

Step 3: Evaluate Tough Choices

Once again, revisit the past and consider the challenging decisions you've had to make, the fears you've faced, and how you overcame them.

Step 4: Revisit and Regroup

Go back to the original value you wrote on sticky notes in step 1 and divide them into five main groups, then select two of the top values for each category. Once you have divided them, give yourself one minute to eliminate seven values until you are only left with three.

Step 5: Reflect on Your Values

The three values left reflect the three values you hold most dear to you. Reflect on how they make you feel if there were any surprises, and if they truly capture what matters most to you (Razzetti, 2020).

EXERCISE: UNEARTHING YOUR INTERESTS

The goal of this exercise is to capture your initial thoughts and feelings about your interests. Follow the exercise in chronological order below:

1. **Word Association:** Write the first 5 words that come to mind that you associate with your interests.
2. **Daydreaming exercise:** Give yourself five minutes. Close your eyes and imagine your ideal day without limitations. What activities are you doing? Where are you? Who are you with? Write down a paragraph summarizing what you imagined.
3. **Quick list:** Give yourself one minute to list 10 things you are passionate about, that bring you joy and capture your interest. For instance, activities, subjects, places, or experiences.
4. **Role models and inspirations:** Identify three people (real or fictional) you admire. Why do you admire them?

5. **Five-year-old you:** Think back to when you were five years old and list down as many activities, hobbies, places, or experiences as you can. Are you still passionate about any of these today?

6. **Personal values connection:** From your list of 10 in the third exercise, pick three that most interest you, then see if they match your three most personal values. How do your favorite activities align with what you find important in life?

Review your responses and look for patterns or recurring themes that can provide insights into your interests.

SETTING SMART GOALS FOR TEENS

SMART is a goal-setting framework that removes uncertainty, grounds us in reality, offers a clear path to achieve our goals with measurable steps, and provides a timeline. It's a roadmap towards our goal, where every step counts, and, of course, it's easy enough to readjust our plan if we stray off course. Think of it as a compass that keeps our eye on the prize!

The *SMART* acronym stands for:

1. **Specific**: Make your goals as clear as possible. For instance, instead of saying, "Stop comparing myself to others on social media," say, "I want to cut down on my time spent on Instagram and Facebook, as these platforms cause me anxiety due to comparing myself to others."

2. **Measurable**: This step is in place to ensure you can track and measure your progress.

3. **Achievable**: Setting a goal that is too difficult can be discouraging. Aim high, but be realistic in your endeavors.

4. **Relevant**: Your goals should be tailored to you and applicable to your unique needs. For instance, "I want to improve my self-esteem and emotional well-being. Since social media contributes to my tendency to compare myself, reducing online comparisons will improve how I view myself and help break the habit of comparing myself to others."
5. **Time-bound**: Give yourself a deadline to keep you focused and motivated. It helps you stay focused and motivated. (Boogaard, 2021)

ALICE'S SMART GOAL

Meet Alice. Alice has started a new school year in a class full of students she doesn't know. She wants to feel more socially confident and make new friends. Her goal is to form new relationships with her classmates and gradually enhance her social confidence in a variety of scenarios.

Specific: Alice aims to make four new friends by the end of the month by initiating introductions, actively engaging with classmates, holding longer conversations, and participating in discussions.

Measurable: Alice wants to engage in or initiate at least one conversation every second day to make one friend a week, totaling four new friends by the end of the month.

Achievable: Alice will start slowly with small talk, expressing her opinions, and gradually increase her involvement in conversations as her comfort level increases with each interaction.

Relevant: Alice wants to make new friends; however, social interactions scare her. To overcome these fears, she needs to build her social confidence.

Time-bound: Alice aims to complete her goal in one month.

Alice utilized *SMART* goals to improve her self-confidence by tailoring her goals to be specific, measurable, achievable, relevant, and time-bound. Ultimately, these parameters helped her track her progress and increase her likelihood of achieving her desired goals.

THE PROCESS OF BREAKING DOWN BIG GOALS

We all know people who set new-year resolutions, but how many people achieve them? Only 10%! That means 90% of individuals who set their goal for the new year ultimately fail, but why is that? (Rissanen, 2022)

It's because they went in without a plan of action; they didn't break their yearly goal into bite-sized, manageable goals with actionable steps. This doesn't only apply to New Year's resolutions; it applies to any big goal. We need to learn to prioritize our goals by learning how to manage our time and gradually progress with small wins to keep us motivated so that we can reach the ultimate prize in the end.

The process of breaking down big goals into smaller, manageable steps is simple but requires discipline. Follow these steps to break down your goals into more manageable pieces.

Step 1: Utilize Smart to Clearly State Your Goal

- Be more self-compassionate and kinder to me in the next 2 months. This is our goal.

Step 2: Break Larger Goals Into Sub-Goals

- Identify and challenge any negative self-talk habits
- Incorporate self-care habits into daily life

- Be realistic and set manageable expectations for yourself
- Learn to let go and forgive your mistakes

Step 3: Actionable Measures to Take to Achieve Subgoals

- Replace negative self-talk with positive affirmations. Identify and reframe at least one negative thought daily for a week.
- Utilize self-care routines to improve your mindset and how you view yourself; practice mindfulness exercises for at least 15 minutes a day; get adequate rest; exercise; and do activities that bring you joy.
- Set achievable goals that you can realistically meet. Setting unrealistic goals will only bring you down when you can't achieve them, and being kinder to yourself will have the opposite effect. Set and meet realistic goals without overburdening yourself for a month.
- Forgive and let go of your mistakes by focusing on the lessons you can learn from them rather than wallowing in them.

Step 4: Make a To-Do-List

- Record your negative thoughts in a journal to record, track, and challenge thoughts, and identify any patterns or trends.
- Make a self-care timetable for the week. Schedule activities such as exercise, meditation, art, or any other activity or exercise that calms and relaxes you.
- Track your goals and ascertain if you are being fair to yourself. Ensure that tasks are not too big and that you are realistic in your abilities in achieving them.
- Reflect on your mistakes. Write down what you can learn from them, and consciously forgive yourself. We all make

mistakes; we are humans.

Step 5: Plan and Prioritize

Ascertain the most important tasks that need to be completed first, and then go down the list from there, starting from most important to least important. Plan according to your hierarchy of tasks.

- For the next two weeks, focus on identifying and reframing your thoughts from negative to positive.
- In weeks three and four, continue to focus on reframing your negative thoughts but also incorporate self-care activities into your routine.
- From Week 5 onwards, continue everything from weeks one to four and start to practice letting go of self-blame and forgiving yourself for your mistakes; instead, learn from them.

Step 6: Track Your Progress

Throughout your journey, incorporate daily and weekly reviews. For daily reviews, note all positive self-talk instances and how well you did with your self-care routine for the day.

For weekly reviews, objectively view your progress realistically and forgive yourself for any perceived shortcomings. Even the tiniest of improvements is a success, even if it doesn't seem like it at the time.

Step 7: Celebrate

Celebrate every success you overcome; this could be on a daily or weekly basis, but don't forget to acknowledge and reward yourself for your progress. This will keep you motivated and foster a more positive relationship with yourself (Everyday Design, 2022).

ADJUSTING YOUR GOALS

As much as the world around us and circumstances change, so do we as people, and our goals are sometimes altered as a result. This is a completely natural part of any goal-setting process. Do not view altering your goals as a setback but rather as a strategic response to evolving circumstances.

Here is how we can modify our goals.

1. **Analyze your current situation:** Determine your current stance in relation to what your original goal was. Identify the changes in your priorities, external factors, and circumstances that made you consider altering your original objective.
2. **Redefine your goal, but make it smart**: Your goal may change, but it still needs to remain a smart goal. Redefine the parameters of your original goal based on your current circumstances and aspirations.
3. **Revaluate steps:** Ascertain if there are any major steps and milestones to achieve your new goal. Determine if your original goals need to be completely reassessed or if they just need to be slightly altered.
4. **Determine new or altered sub-goals:** Based on your new steps, identify the necessary sub-goals you need to achieve based on your ultimate, larger goal. Again, these may need

to be completely changed or altered depending on the extent to which your new goal differs from your original goal.

5. **Update your tasks:** Update your to-do list to align with your new or altered goal.

6. **Reprioritize and replan:** Prioritize your new tasks based on how they will impact your overall goal and sub-goals. Reassess your timeline if necessary, and ensure your plan is adaptable to unexpected events.

7. **Track revised progress:** Regularly monitor your progress against the modified sub-goals. Celebrate achievements to stay motivated.

8. **Reflect and learn:** Reflect on the adjustments you have made and learn from the process. Being flexible, adaptable, and maintaining a growth mindset is crucial as we alter our goals.

JESSICA WATSON: THE 16-YEAR-OLD WHO ACHIEVED HER GOAL OF SAILING SOLO ACROSS THE GLOBE

In her astonishing solo circumnavigation around the globe at just 16, Australian-born Jessica Watson showcased to the world the transformative impact our goals have on our lives. This ambitious teen navigated the vast expanses of the world's oceans with a meticulous compass of objectives, ensuring that she would not only succeed in her audacious journey but also prioritize her safety in the process.

Jessica's overarching goals acted as guiding beacons and were illuminated through the strategic breakdown of her goals into manageable milestones. These milestones ranged from specific routes to supply management, boat maintenance, and fortifying her mental and emotional well-being throughout her journey.

Her unwavering determination and focus to succeed in her goals became the wind in her sails, which steered her through adversity and challenges by effectively managing setbacks. Jessica Watson became the youngest person to solo circumnavigate the globe, which is a testament to the potency of determination and strategic planning in goal-setting. Her story shows the world that we are capable of anything if we set the right goals and are prepared to do what it takes to achieve them. (Inspire Speakers, 2020)

OVERCOMING OBSTACLES TO YOUR GOALS

Our teenage years are a vulnerable time in our lives; we are forced to navigate a challenging growth era both physically and emotionally, marked by hormonal changes, puberty, and societal pressures. Teens often feel misunderstood and struggle to overcome obstacles such as self-esteem struggles, stress, anxiety, depression, bullying, online comparison, parental expectations, academic pressure, and being influenced by peers. While many teens face one or more of these issues, there are measures we can adopt to help overcome this obstacle:

Don't Think Worst-Case Scenario

Firstly, collect your thoughts, find your rhythm, and maintain your composure. Identify what is causing your anxiety, and understand that when we feel overwhelmed, we limit our ability to think clearly. More often than not, our anxiety stems from imagining the worst-case scenario, which is rarely the result.

Two Magic Questions

These two magic words help us gain a rational perspective of the challenges we face:

Question One: Is This a Real Threat/Hinderance or Not?

When we can determine if something is a real threat or simply a challenging obstacle that we can overcome through perseverance, it helps prevent "fight or flight," which hinders our problem-solving abilities.

Question Two: Is This Problem Temporary?

Assess whether the problem at hand is a long-term issue or a short-term obstacle to overcome. This will assist us in gaining perspective on our future feelings. Continually remind yourself that challenges are transient and do not last forever.

Turn Mountains Into Molehills

Just like we can break down goals into smaller, more achievable segments, we can break down our challenges into smaller, more manageable pieces we can overcome. This makes our challenges feel more achievable and helps boost our confidence as we slowly start to regain control of the situation.

Utilize Strategies to Simplify the Obstacle

These three essential strategies help simplify the obstacles we face:

Strategy One: Don't Say "Never." Say, "Not yet."

This simple change in phrase replaces self-defeating thoughts with a positive outlook, emphasizing that with time and effort, we can overcome challenges. View limitations as opportunities to grow.

Strategy Two: Climb the Easy Hills First

By addressing solvable aspects of the problem first, we will gain momentum and confidence.

Strategy Three: Change Perspectives

Consider adopting a new perspective on the obstacle. Challenge yourself to view it from a different angle, or ask your friends and family for their advice; perhaps their perspective on the matter can give you insights to solve your problem.

If we follow these steps, we can overcome any obstacle in front of our goals (Center for Parent and Teen Communication, 2022).

STAYING MOTIVATED AND SEEKING HELP FROM OTHERS

Motivation is the key to achieving what we set out to do. It's one thing to set goals, but if we aren't motivated to complete them, then we never will. Firstly, what is motivation? Motivation is the process that instigates, directs, and sustains goal-oriented behaviors. (Cherry, 2023). Motivation is fueled by our desires, achievements, setbacks, and past experiences. Notice the resemblance to the factors driving self-confidence.

Understanding motivation is one thing, but finding and maintaining motivation can be challenging but not impossible. For starters, we need to set *SMART* goals and break them down into manageable sub-sectors that are achievable and realistic. Motivation is a momentum game; it is crucial that we integrate our goals into our daily routines, monitor our progress regularly, practice mindfulness, and adopt self-compassion.

We also cannot ignore the importance of seeking support and guidance from others. Take inspiration from people you admire, and seek support from your support system and other supportive sources you trust. Remember that setbacks are inevitable. We cannot lose motivation every time something goes wrong; we need to be flexible, adaptive, and resilient in the face of changing circumstances. If we stay true to ourselves, persevere, and celebrate milestones, we can foster and maintain motivation (Healthdirect Australia, 2022).

Goals are integral to providing us with direction, but getting to know ourselves on a deeper level is what truly draws up the map.

SELF DISCOVERY AND IDENTITY

"I am who I am. Not who you think I am. Not who you want me to be. I am me."

— BRIGITTE NICOLE

WHO AM I?

Who am I? I am sure we have all asked ourselves this question, which should be easy to answer. I mean, who knows us better than ourselves? Yet, it all too often perplexes us and remains unanswered. This seemingly straightforward question is wrapped in layers upon layers of complexity, prompting introspection and contemplation, something that often feels uncomfortable and unnatural to us.

When we ask, "Who am I?" we grapple with multifaceted layers of identity shaped by experiences, values, relationships, and aspirations. Decoding the mysteries of ourselves requires us to navigate uncertainties and contradictions, propelling us on a nonstop journey of self-discovery and identity.

THE IMPORTANCE OF SELF-REFLECTION

Self-reflection essentially involves dedicating time to deeply evaluate and assess our thoughts, attitudes, desires, and motivations. In essence, it is asking ourselves the big question, "Why do we feel and act this way?"

With self-reflection, we gain insights into our strengths as well as an understanding of what is holding us back, so we can make the necessary changes to grow as individuals. This introspective process reduces our risk of being trapped in unproductive and uninspiring routines (Perry, 2022).

Taking a moment in our day to objectively look at ourselves and ask questions like "Am I being kind to myself?" nudges us on a journey of self-discovery and guides us on a path of personal growth.

Below are some of my favorite self-reflection questions:

1. Am I making the most of my time?
2. Do I appreciate what I have, and what am I taking for granted?
3. Am I adopting a positive perspective?
4. Am I staying true to myself?
5. What matters most to me?
6. What can I do to take better care of myself?
7. What makes me uncomfortable or frightens me?
8. When was the last time I left my comfort zone?
9. What aspects of my life am I content with?
10. Am I waking up each morning prepared to be energized for the day ahead?

11. Am I thinking positive thoughts before I go to bed?
12. Am I investing effort in my relationships?
13. Am I prioritizing my physical well-being?
14. Am I letting go of stress over things out of my control?
15. Am I making consistent progress toward my goals?

UNDERSTANDING OUR PERSONALITY TRAITS

Our personality traits shape who we are as individuals. When we begin to understand and recognize our unique characteristics, behaviors, and tendencies, we are better suited to answer the lingering question on our minds: "Who am I?"

This is not as difficult as one may think, and that is due to a widely accepted personality trait framework known as *OCEAN*, otherwise known as the Big Five personality traits. This model recognizes that five major personality traits can accurately categorize human personalities. The acronym *OCEAN* represents the five major dimensions of openness, conscientiousness, extraversion, agreeableness, and neuroticism:

Openness

- Characterized by imagination and insight
- Open and eager to learn and experience new things
- Has a broad range of interests
- Are often very creative and exhibit abstract thinking
- Open to accepting and exploring unconventional ideas

Conscientiousness

- Known for thoughtfulness.
- Exhibits great impulse control

- Associated with goal-directed behaviors
- Known to be detail-oriented and organized
- Excel in structured environments
- They plan ahead and take into consideration how their behavior and actions impact others.

Extraversion

- Known for their sociability and assertiveness
- Excel in social interactions
- They gain energy from being around other people
- They enjoy attention

Agreeableness

- Known for their trust, kindness, and selflessness
- Exhibit high amounts of empathy and prosocial behaviors (helping others, sharing, donating, cooperating, volunteering, etc.)
- Pursues careers in helping others, such as charity work, medicine, or mental health practitioners.

Neuroticism

- Associated with moodiness and emotional instability
- Have a heightened response to stress
- Prone to anxiety and mood swings
- This trait is not indicative of anti-social behavior but reflects an emotional response to stress.

Utilizing the OCEAN framework and embracing the nuances of human personality helps us understand how we navigate the world, make choices, and interact with others (Jayson Darby, 2022).

THE INFLUENCE OF FAMILY, CULTURE, AND SOCIETY

Our identity is complex and is often shaped by external factors, some of which shape our very identity before we even ascertain human consciousness. Three major factors intricately shaping us are our family, culture, and society.

From the very beginning of our existence, society has shaped our identity through categorization and labeling based on traits and desired behaviors we are expected to abide by, influencing who we become.

Our family also plays an extremely prominent role in shaping our identity. They are the first people we interact with as infants. Those encounters with our parents, siblings, and extended family members during our formative years significantly contribute, both consciously and unconsciously, to constructing the foundational aspect of our sense of self.

Lastly, our culture is profoundly linked to how we perceive ourselves and engage with the world. Our culture, race, and ethnicity imbue us with unique beliefs, experiences, and traditions, influencing our language, shaping our values, and providing us with a sense of belonging.

In essence, the influence of society, family, and culture on our sense of self is a complex and continuous process, with each element playing its part in constructing the multifaceted nature of who we are (AlSabbah, 2020).

EMBRACING OUR UNIQUENESS

 "In order to be irreplaceable, one must always be different."

— COCO CHANEL

Recently, I went to watch an incredible orchestra play live at a concert, and it got me thinking. Collectively, the orchestra played a harmonious masterpiece, but each player was responsible for their distinctive sound and notes to create a beautiful melody. Life is like an orchestra. Every person on the planet has their own equally unique and significant qualities that contribute to the richness of this word. In the symphony of life, our uniqueness adds such depth and beauty to the world around us, highlighting the importance of our unique contributions to the world.

Think of it like this: if we were all to wear denim jeans and a black t-shirt every day till the end of time, there would be no difference between one another, and we would not grow as individuals nor help society evolve. We need to embrace our uniqueness and develop an identity that we can feel proud of.

Taking the time to understand ourselves and discover what makes us unique helps us feel important, purposeful, happy, and truly connected with ourselves and others.

Embrace your unique identity by utilizing these tips:

- Accept yourself for your strengths and your weaknesses. It is difficult to know who we truly are if we refuse what makes us unique.
- Explore other people's stories to understand your narrative
- Do not compromise on your authentic self.

- Forge a community of like-minded people with similar interests and values
- Acknowledge and embrace your talents and skills for what they are
- Resist the pressure to conform and stay true to your beliefs
- Pursue activities that bring you joy, not just obligations
- See constructive criticism as a valuable opportunity to grow (Prasad, 2015)

IDENTITY EXPLORATION WORKSHEET

Understanding ourselves is crucial for personal development. Use this worksheet to help you explore various factors of your identity:

Self-Reflection

1.1. List your unique qualities, talents, and interests (5 points for each one).

1.2. How do you think others perceive you?

1.3. Do you challenge expressing your true self? If so, why?

Family and Cultural Influences

2.1 Explore ways in which your family influences your identity.

2.2 What cultural traditions and values are important to you?

2.3 Do you feel pressure to conform to certain expectations from your family or culture?

Social Circle

3.1. Describe your friendships and social interactions.

3.2. Do you feel accepted by your peers and others around you?

3.3. Do your friends influence your identity? If so, how?

Personal Beliefs and Values

4.1. List down your core beliefs and values (3 points for each).

4.2. Have your values and beliefs changed over time? If so, how?

Interests and Passions

5.1. What interests bring you joy and fulfillment?

5.2. In what ways do these interests contribute to how you view yourself?

5.3. Are there any new activities or passions you would like to explore?

Challenges and Growth Opportunities

6.1. What past experiences, good or bad, have shaped your identity?

6.2. How have you grown from these experiences?

6.3. What current obstacles are holding you back from embracing your identity?

Create Your Identity Statement

7.1. Consider all your answers above and write a paragraph that reflects your understanding of your identity.

THE ROLE OF VALUES IN DECISION-MAKING

At the end of the day, we are all empty vessels when we first come into this world; however, that empty space quickly fills when we adopt our core values and beliefs to shape who we are.

"It's not hard to make decisions when you know what your values are." These are the wise words of Roy Disney, and he is absolutely correct. Once we embrace this fundamental truth, our values will guide effective decisions, and we will be able to recognize our uniqueness and our individual purposes. When we make decisions, it is natural to seek advice from others, especially for significant decisions in life, but ultimately, the ownership of the decisions we make rests with us. Therefore, instead of being swayed by our emotions and the opinions of others, trust your rational judgment and stay true to your values.

Consider these three key factors to assist you in making crucial decisions that align with your values:

Utilize Principles To Guide Decisions

Our principles—the fundamental truths—construct the foundation of our behaviors and beliefs. For instance, if the principle of being a responsible member of society rings true for you, then it is natural that your actionable decisions would reflect something in line with civic duty. Aligning our choices with our principles gives us a sense of peace of mind and helps us stay true to ourselves (Bacon, 2020).

Decide by Using Standards

Evaluate your choices against the standards you have established for yourself. Evaluate what you stand for and what your non-negotiables are to help guide you in making decisions. For instance, if honesty is one of your non-negotiables, evaluate if your decision aligns with your standards and if you are being true to yourself.

Consider The Degree of Importance When Making Decisions

Consider the different aspects of the decision, and then utilize your principles and standards as a benchmark to organize the hierarchy of importance. Imagine we had to prioritize choices that relate to education, friendships, and our personal growth. The degree of importance we assign to each of these decisions will differ from person to person but will be based on an individual's values (Mind Tools, 2022b).

OUR BELIEFS SHAPE OUR ACTIONS

Beliefs shape our reality and, in turn, motivate our actions. The transformative power of our beliefs lies in the realization that the seemingly impossible becomes possible through sheer belief in its potential to become achievable. When we align our thoughts with positive beliefs, we take the necessary actions required to shape our reality, regardless of whether the odds don't seem to be in our favor.

Our beliefs directly influence our thoughts, and our thoughts influence our actions. Think of it this way: if you wholeheartedly believe in your abilities and feel you deserve to get into your dream college, you are far more likely to seek out opportunities to make that dream happen actively. This isn't a matter of being over-confident; it is about believing in your potential to attend the college of your dreams and pushing yourself to navigate the college application process with greater motivation, assurance, and self-belief.

On the other hand, if we believe that goals are unattainable, this can be a self-fulfilling prophecy of failure. If you tell yourself that your dream college is out of reach, chances are you won't take the necessary steps or have the confidence in yourself to turn that dream into a reality.

Our beliefs serve as the foundation for our assumptions about life. They set the rules and establish the framework of what is right and wrong, what is impossible, and what is possible. They guide the feasibility of our aspirations.

So remember, don't say, "I'm not sure if this will work out." Say, "This will work out because I will make it work out!" (Batra, 2019).

CHALLENGING AND REFINING OUR BELIEFS

Challenging or refining our beliefs is natural as we evolve as individuals. However, we often stubbornly hold onto outdated beliefs and are reluctant to acknowledge that they are no longer valid or relevant. This could be because we have grown as people, evolved our mindsets, adopted different perspectives, or experienced changing external circumstances in our lives. In essence, often our beliefs have passed their expiration date. The problem of not refining or challenging our beliefs as we grow can hinder our personal growth and prevent the adoption of more accurate perspectives.

When we reevaluate our beliefs, we should listen without judgment. Avoid judging other people's beliefs before hearing them out and completely understanding their point of view, and prioritize understanding before being understood ourselves. By engaging with others and gaining a deeper understanding of their beliefs, we may gain insight into our own.

Consider conflicting views. Even if someone's beliefs go against yours, that doesn't mean you shouldn't expose yourself to diverse sources of information. Engage in debates and ask questions, as this will further help us understand both our beliefs and those of others. Lastly, and perhaps most importantly, confront your own self-limiting beliefs that align with your personal capabilities.

Conquer your fear; don't run from it. To unravel fears, recognize them as false evidence appearing real (FEAR). Unlocking our full potential requires a thorough analysis and assessment of what is genuinely real, ensuring our personal growth and development (Millen, 2022).

FINDING YOUR PASSION AND INTERESTS

 "No alarm clock is needed. My passion wakes me."

— ERIC THOMAS

Our passions and interests are what give us direction and purpose. They guide us to better understand ourselves, give us a reason to get out of bed in the morning, and help us lead fulfilling lives. Refer back to Chapter 7 for the exercise on uncovering your values. If you feel the need to question or challenge your values, revisit and redo the exercise for a thorough exploration.

THE DIFFERENCE BETWEEN HOBBIES AND PASSIONS

Hobbies and passions may seem similar on the surface, but there is one key distinction that sets them apart. A hobby is an activity we do to pursue feelings of enjoyment during our leisure time. In contrast, passion is what lights our inner fire and drives us in our enduring pursuit of what gets us motivated, which we willingly engage in consistently.

For instance, someone who paints on the weekends for a few hours is engaging in a hobby. However, if they were dedicating countless hours, consistently learning new art techniques, and were enrolled in a couple of art course lessons as they dreamed of turning their artistic talent into a career that would be a passion (Hasa, 2020).

Hobbies vs Passions

Hobby	Passion
An activity done regularly and casually during their off time	Continually and relentlessly pursuing an activity with strong enthusiasm and excitement with the goal of mastery and fulfillment.
The aim is to have fun and engage with it when you have the time	The goal is to engage in it consistently out of love and a desire for mastery, making it a daily practice and enjoyment.
good way to fill up free time	You can't imagine living without it

(Hasa, 2020)

HOW TO DISCOVER OUR PASSIONS

Now that we know that our passions are the gasoline that lights our hearts ablaze, we need to find out what our passions really are. Luckily, there are six magic questions we can ask ourselves to simplify our search. These questions guide unraveling our genuine passion for life and aligning our pursuit with authentic self-fulfillment!

Question 1: What Makes You So Engrossed in Something That You Lose Track of Time?

This could be a pastime like singing, a sport, or something from your childhood that you used to do for hours on end. It may seem like a hobby now, but think of how you can turn that into something you could do as a career or energize you to grow as an individual.

Question 2: What Topics or Subjects Make You a Total Chatterbox Where You Could Talk for Hours Without Getting Bored?

A passion isn't just what gets you up in the morning; it's what lights your soul. Perhaps you can talk about film till the end of time, or you love a good debate about music, or flowers light up your world.

Question 3: What do you Want to be Remembered as? What Legacy Do You Want to Leave Behind?

Maybe you want to be remembered as the first female head coach for a male NFL franchise, or you want to put on a show on Broadway that will be talked about for generations to come.

Question 4: If You Had All The Money in the World, How Would You Envision a Day In Your Financially Secure Future?

Maybe you'd love to see the world and experience different cultures. Maybe you'd want to sell a bestselling novel. Or maybe you'd like to give back to the community and help others.

Question 5: What Fulfills You in Your Current Life?

Maybe it's being in control of all your schoolwork. It could be that helping your classmates succeed makes you feel fulfilled. Perhaps being the captain of the basketball team brings you a sense of purpose and joy.

Question 6: What is Holding You Back?

This question helps identify what we want less of in our lives. It could be comparing yourself negatively to others on social media. It could be following a goal that doesn't align with your values. Or it could be engaging in activities to impress others (Dowches-Wheeler, 2023).

Consider your answers to these questions carefully. Identify recurring patterns and distill what genuinely excites you. Explore ways to channel that excitement into a passion that aligns with your interests and aspirations.

BALANCING VARIOUS INTERESTS

Many people find that exploring multiple interests is highly beneficial as it allows them to experiment with different passions and develop a myriad of skill groups; however, it can be overwhelming at times. If you find yourself juggling too many interests at once, don't stress; take a step back and assess your situation. Here's what you do:

1. Make a list of all your different interests and prioritize them in order of importance, considering what you aspire to achieve the most.
2. Develop a schedule and allocate set times for each interest

3. Adhere to this schedule strictly and be realistic about how you allocate time and deadlines
4. Break larger interests or tasks into smaller ones
5. Reward yourself and remember to take breaks
6. Be flexible and allow for changes in your schedule (Occo London, 2023)

THE ROLE OF CURIOSITY IN SELF-DISCOVERY

Curiosity plays an important role in our journey of self-discovery as it sparks our excitement to explore new experiences, thus unveiling hidden joys and understanding within ourselves. It's important to realize that curiosity is not an innate trait we are born with, but one we can develop over time and with practice.

As we engage with the world and ourselves, curiosity becomes a more natural part of who we are. The more curious we are, the more questions we will ask and the more interest we will show in others. Therefore, people will feel more valued and more willing to open up to us, creating stronger internal and external bonds (Campbell, 2019).

It is essential to know ourselves inside and out, but it is just as important to cultivate strong, healthy, relationships with others!

BUILDING HEALTHY RELATIONSHIPS

L ife is like a beautiful garden filled with stunningly vibrant flowers of relationships. Just as gardeners lovingly nurture their plants, we must also tend to and care for the relationships we build. Together, we will embark on a journey of exploration as we uncover the art of protecting our metaphorical garden. Every interaction we have with others has the potential to blossom into something beautiful and fulfilling.

Commitment

Commitment is what initiates any relationship; however, sustaining a healthy one requires continual effort and investment. A relationship is not the answer to a personal issue but rather is about a mutual commitment to individual growth and shared well-being. Laziness or the expectation that one partner should bring everything to the table will often lead to disillusionment and resentment.

Communication

Communication is the beating heart of a relationship and is a dynamic exchange that requires both partners to speak truthfully and listen receptively. When communication breaks down in a relationship, it is often due to personal challenges, such as a history of ridicule, verbal abuse, or fear of rejection. When there is a broken link in the chain of communication, honest expression can become difficult. Avoiding communication hampers our ability to connect with others, solve problems, and ultimately contribute to a failed relationship.

Honesty

Honesty is the key to building a foundation of trust, respect, and compassion with others. Dishonesty is influenced by the fear of the consequences of telling the truth or the desire to control. Side-stepping or fabricating the truth creates a wedge between others and pushes people away from us.

If we choose to ignore these relationship cornerstones, we may over rely on others for love and support, weakening the foundation until it crumbles (Sacred Journeys, 2021).

BUILDING TRUST THROUGH HONESTY AND INTEGRITY

Building trust takes time and consistent effort. It requires qualities such as patience, understanding, open communication, and, most importantly, honesty and integrity. For instance, couples who open up to each other and share their thoughts and feelings honestly will build a richer connection than those who withhold information from one another.

Consider these tips to cultivate trust through honesty and integrity:

Tip One: Embrace Truthfulness

When we are true to others and ourselves, we fortify respect for each other and place more value on the relationship.

Tip Two: Acknowledge Mistakes

Admit when you are wrong and take responsibility for your mistakes. Making mistakes is not the end of the world, but avoiding them can be a deal-breaker. When we accept accountability and take responsibility, we foster openness and a stronger relationship.

Tip Four: Promise-Keeping

Keep promises to the best of your ability, as this is crucial to building a foundation of trust. However, life is unpredictable, and sometimes, we are not able to keep our promises for reasons beyond our control. In these circumstances, it is vital to be honest and communicate the reasons for not fulfilling our promises to foster understanding and trust in our relationship.

Tip Four: Be Consistent

Being consistent with our actions and words reinforces our dependability.

Overall, open and honest communication is key to fostering transparency in a relationship. It illustrates our genuine consideration for other people's thoughts and feelings, resulting in stronger relationships (Faster Capital, 2022).

EFFECTIVE COMMUNICATION IN RELATIONSHIPS

Relationships are beautiful and extremely fulfilling, but that doesn't mean they don't come with their fair share of conflicts. The challenge does not exist in the conflict itself, but rather in how we manage it. Ineffective communication in times of conflict can lead to misunderstandings, disagreements, resentment, and anger, creating distance between people.

To build resilient and healthy relationships, consider the following:

Be Empathetic and Listen to Their Point-of-View

When faced with criticism, don't respond with emotion; instead, practice empathetic and active listening. Pay attention to their point of view without immediately responding. This will help you better understand the situation, stop you from emotionally lashing out, force you to consider differing perspectives, and guide you in responding empathetically. This will facilitate calm and effective communication.

Avoid Accusatory Language

Express your feelings using "I" instead of "you." Instead of saying "You were rude," say "I feel like you were being rude just now." This helps draw attention to people's mistakes without triggering a defensive response.

Compromise is Key

A relationship involves a joint effort. Seek solutions that meet everyone's needs; prioritize compromise rather than winning an argument. For example, a couple might find that one of them prefers to spend their nights out with other people, while the other prefers to be alone with their partner. They compromise by alternating between one weekend going out to social events and the next weekend staying in and watching a movie together, then continuing that process.

Take a Time-Out, But Don't Let it Fester

When emotions are escalating, it may be a good idea to cool off and just do your own thing for a while. Go for a walk or take a nap, but make sure you return to resolve the conflict when you both have a clear mind. Letting the conflict fester for too long makes it harder to resolve (Scott, 2022).

COMMUNICATION BARRIERS

Teenagers of today face numerous challenges, and thus numerous communication barriers arise as they venture forth on their journey of self-discovery. They are experiencing a vulnerable time in their lives; their perception of themselves constantly evolves, making opening up and communicating challenging for many teens. Here's why:

Feeling Embarrassed to Show Vulnerability

Many teens feel embarrassed or that they are being a burden if they discuss their struggles with others. They fear discussing their challenges may be seen as a form of inadequacy or weakness. As a result, they may not feel comfortable or know how to ask for help from others.

Anxiety and Stress

The taxing demands of teens to excel academically, navigate social situations, and meet external standards can lead to overwhelming feelings of anxiety, hindering their ability to respond effectively. Many find solace in silence as a way to self-soothe during this challenging period.

Fear of Disappointing Others and Expecting a Negative Reaction

Teenagers often feel that if they open up about their problems, they may end up disappointing those they respect and love, thus avoiding open communication. Beyond fearing disappointment, teens often predict a negative response from others before they have even engaged in conversation.

Lack of Trust

Teenagers are at a vulnerable time in their lives and often struggle to trust others more than most. Teens often refrain from engaging in open and honest conversations if they don't trust you.

Past Experiences

If teens feel that past experiences have led to negative consequences, they often refrain from conversation as they deem it a safer alternative (Hudson, 2022).

Understanding teenage communication barriers is only the beginning; let's explore the measures we can take to overcome them:

- Consider an appropriate time and place to engage in a conversation. Ensure that you select a distraction-free location.
- Utilize simple, understandable, and clear language
- Use active listening and engage intensively
- Don't overload somebody with questions; convey one message at a time.
- Be respectful, and understand that if somebody chooses not to communicate, that is their choice.
- Confirm a person's understanding when you communicate
- Acknowledge, respect, and adapt to the emotional and non-verbal responses they exhibit

COMMUNICATION AND TRUST BUILDING EXERCISE: MINEFIELD

For this exercise, you need at least two people, a blindfold, obstacles to create a "minefield," and some space for navigation. Once you set up your obstacles, blindfold one partner and bring them into the room; they are not allowed to see the room once the obstacles have been put in place.

The challenge begins as the partner who isn't blindfolded guides their blindfolded partner throughout the minefield using only verbal communication. No touching is allowed to aid navigation! The success of this exercise lies in the blindfolded partner's trust and the other partner's ability to communicate effectively.

While frustration and maybe a stubbed toe may arise, this exercise is a fun way to highlight communication strengths and weaknesses and instill trust in one another. Once completed, each partner will switch roles, and the obstacles will need to be reset (Ackerman, 2019).

BOUNDARIES AND RESPECT

No matter the relationship, whether it be romantic, platonic, friendly, or familial, maintaining healthy boundaries is essential for creating healthy relationships, building trust, enhancing self-worth, and improving overall well-being.

When I was in my first year of college, I struggled to balance my time between my studies, working part-time, volunteering, and maintaining a social life. My time wasn't my own, and I was beginning to feel completely overwhelmed.

I soon realized I felt this way because I struggled to say "no." Thus, I decided to set boundaries for myself, limit my work hours, and be more selective with how I spent my time. It was difficult at first to say "no" to aspects of my life I so often said "yes" to, but over time, it began to feel more natural. I noticed that the more I honored the boundaries I set for myself, the more my overall well-being improved. This simple tweak allowed me to focus more on my studies and invest time in building meaningful relationships.

THE IMPORTANCE OF SETTING HEALTHY BOUNDARIES

Boundaries can be best understood as invisible lines in the sand that we draw up for ourselves. They define what is acceptable and what isn't when engaging with ourselves and others. Boundaries are crucial to prioritizing our needs over the need to please others.

There are several kinds of boundaries, such as:

Emotional Boundaries

"I'm not comfortable discussing that" is a perfectly suitable and respectful response. Protect yourself from engaging in sensitive topics that you don't wish to discuss or that make you feel uncomfortable. These boundaries preserve and safeguard your emotional well-being.

Material Boundaries

Boundaries that dictate your comfort levels regarding your personal belongings. Asking for the laptop you lent to a friend back because it took them too long to return it is completely acceptable and something you shouldn't feel guilty about.

Physical Boundaries

This ascertains your comfort levels regarding physical interactions, such as excessive hugging, touching, or evasion of your personal space. This filters through to sexual boundaries, which draw the line on any sexual behavior that makes you feel uncomfortable.

Time Boundaries

This relates to how you choose to spend your time. These boundaries help foster a healthy work-life balance. For instance, prioritizing homework and limiting social activities during the week will ensure sufficient rest and academic focus. However, when it isn't exam season, you may spend more time with your friends and less time hitting the books.

Relationship Boundaries

Relationship boundaries govern how we connect with others and are a mash-up of emotional, physical, time, and even material boundaries. Boundaries for different kinds of relationships will differ, but it is vital that we respect each other's boundaries to form healthy relationships.

Through setting and adhering to these different boundaries, we will:

- Safeguard our emotional wellbeing
- Protect our physical comfort levels
- Distinguishing personal thoughts, feelings, and needs from others'
- Refrain from feeling responsible for other's happiness
- Fortify relationships through mutual respect
- Utilize our time more wisely
- Prevent tension and conflict from arising
- Cultivating a strong sense of identity (Better Help, 2024)

SETTING BOUNDARIES AND HOW TO COMMUNICATE THEM TO OTHERS

Boundaries are essential for our overall well-being, but sometimes they prove challenging to set for ourselves and communicate with others. Boundaries require a great deal of self-awareness, so if you struggle to set boundaries, practice self-reflection and dig deep to find insights about yourself.

The truth is that setting boundaries is only the beginning; the real challenge is communicating our boundaries. This could stem from multiple reasons. We may struggle to communicate our feelings or fear hurting others verbally. We may have a personal history of our boundaries being violated, thus impacting our trust in others when asserting our boundaries. Fear of rejection and judgment is another hurdle many need to overcome when communicating their boundaries. Whatever the reason, we need to communicate our boundaries clearly before resentment and frustration hinder our wellbeing.

These tips will help you set and communicate your boundaries:

- Be clear when stating your boundaries, calmly but assertively, and explain the consequences of what will happen if they are ignored
- Make use of "I" statements to express how others' actions impact you personally. "I feel disrespected when..."
- Make sure you are consistent with your boundaries; don't only enforce them sometimes and not other times
- Keep good company by surrounding yourself with individuals who respect your boundaries
- Take ownership of your boundaries and stay true to them. Don't let people bully you into abandoning them
- Remain non-confrontational, open to questions, and comprise if you feel it benefits everyone involved
- Be firm, set the record straight if your boundary is not up for debate, and don't be afraid to say "no!"
- Prioritize your own needs and desires and trust your instincts (LeClair, 2023).

RESPECTING OTHERS' BOUNDARIES

 "You may not understand why someone has a boundary in place and it may differ from what is acceptable to you. Regardless, each person has a right to set their own limits. Ignoring a boundary is essentially a form of violating someone's rights."

— MEGHAN MARCUM

Mutual respect for each other's boundaries is key to a healthy relationship. Respecting other people's boundaries isn't much different from how you want others to respect yours. Consider these tips:

- Communicate clearly and ask upfront how a person is feeling instead of assuming their comfort level
- Observe non-verbal cues (tone, body language, and their attempts to change the topic); based on this, we will be able to gauge their comfort level
- Accept "no" as an answer
- Don't take the "no" personally; understand that people set boundaries for self-care reasons, not to personally reject people.
- Respect their boundaries, even if you don't understand them. Everybody sets boundaries based on their needs and experiences; it's important to respect these differences.
- Don't act emotionally because somebody is upholding their boundaries
- Respect their autonomy to make their own decisions
- Work on understanding your boundaries to better understand the boundaries of others (Gupta, 2022).

THE ROLE OF MUTUAL RESPECT IN RELATIONSHIPS

A relationship founded on mutual respect is essential to cultivating healthy and fulfilling relationships. It fosters open communication, emotional security, trust, acceptance, and mutual understanding. It is a relationship where everyone experiences satisfaction through active listening, empathy, validation, and mutual support. Ultimately, relationships grounded in mutual respect will benefit from heightened joy and emotional contentment, and an overall sense of well-being will hold the relationship together like glue.

Moreover, conflict resolution will be far smoother. Conflicts are approached with a mindset of listening and compromise, as all parties involved respect each other's perspectives and emotions (Allo Health, 2023).

MAYA STICKS TO HER BOUNDARIES

When Maya was in high school, she was a high-achieving honor student. She had her heart set on going to the college of her dreams and prioritized her academic goals with intensity and commitment. However, at 17 years old, she was at the age where she felt the pervasive influence of peer pressure.

She was a popular girl with many friends and would often get invited to parties that featured underage drinking and substance experimentation. Although these invites seemed tempting as she had a desire to fit in with her classmates, she knew they were not aligned with her values and that this type of behavior would challenge her focus on her end goal. Thus, Maya stood her ground and firmly honored her boundaries by politely declining these social invitations.

Initially, it was challenging, and she was met with skepticism and teasing from her classmates. Despite this, her boundaries never wavered. Over time, Maya's friends and classmates began to admire her steadfast resolve and gain the respect of her peers. Her unwavering dedication to her boundaries inspired her classmates and even influenced others to reevaluate their choices. Maya not only preserved her integrity but also cultivated a culture of mutual respect for individual boundaries.

THE SIGNS OF A SUPPORTIVE RELATIONSHIP

Discovering that you have a relationship (romantic, platonic, or familial) with someone who is supportive, empathetic, encouraging, and there for you when you need them most is one of the greatest joys this world can bring. Supportive relationships run deeper than grand gestures; the true magic behind these relationships lies in the small acts of everyday kindness, the profound respect for each other's uniqueness, and consistent encouragement to help you become the best version of yourself.

Consider these signs of what a supportive relationship looks like:

First Sign: Trust is a Gradual and Reciprocal Process

You support each other, you believe in one another's potential, mutual respect is evident, and you are both each other's biggest cheerleaders.

Second Sign: You Cherish Quality Time Together

You make an active and conscious effort to spend quality time together. It's about the quality of time, not the quantity, and sharing both joyful and challenging moments.

Third Sign: It's a Safe Haven

These relationships make you feel safe in all aspects of life—physically, emotionally, and mentally. You can be yourself without any fear of judgment.

Fourth Sign: Accountability and Apologies

You accept each other's imperfections, admit your mistakes, and you forgive one another. You both own up to your actions, offer genuine apologies, and commit to positive change.

Fifth Sign: Encouragement and Growth

You give each other constructive feedback, celebrate each other's wins, push each other to achieve your goals, and help one another rediscover their passions.

Sixth Sign: You Share the Spotlight

You both ensure your voices are heard and respected. You avoid selfishness and give each other an equal opportunity to shine and express themselves.

Seventh Sign: Open Communication

You both feel comfortable being vulnerable; you reinforce that feelings are valid; and you strive for emotional maturity.

Eighth Sign: Respected Boundaries

You both respect one another's boundaries (Brown, 2023)

THE DO'S AND DON'TS OF BEING A SUPPORTIVE FRIEND

Being a supportive friend often doesn't require us to take immediate or drastic action; rather, it typically requires us to listen and empathize with them, not solve their problems. Ultimately, we can be supportive friends by being present and attentive; in doing so, we are already making a difference. Remember, it's not our job to fix every problem; sometimes, providing support is the most valuable thing we can do for those we care for.

Consider the dos and don'ts of being a supportive friend:

Do's	Don'ts
Empathize with your friend; don't let them know that you understand what they are feeling	Don't make assumptions about their feelings or needs, ask instead.
Validate them by Illustrating understanding and acceptance of their distress	Offer support before solutions. Don't take on the responsibility to "fix it."
Ask Questions and show curiosity to let your friend know that you care about what they are going through	Keep the focus on their experience. Avoid comparing your own problems with theirs.

(Hickey, 2019)

CONNECTION BUILDING EXERCISE: STORY SWAP SCAVENGER HUNT

This is a scavenger hunt with a twist. In this exercise, instead of searching for physical items, partners will share short stories or memories tied to a specific location or object with one another.

Based on the clues given in the stories or memories shared, you will have to find the specific location or object tied to what was shared with you. Each location or item holds personal significance, and it is your job to find out what that place or thing is.

Once you find the specified location or object based on the story given to you, your partner will explain why that location or object is so special to them and how you played a role in making it special. Once done, you will swap roles; the storyteller will become the scavenger, and vice versa This activity not only strengthens connections by learning more about how you both have influenced each other's lives but also adds an element of fun and adventure to the experience.

Building strong and dependable relationships with others is a monumental step, however, we must also learn to navigate the challenges of these newfound relationships.

HANDLING CONFLICT AND REJECTION

C onflict is natural for everybody, but for teenagers, it's even more common.

- 1 in 5 young people say they are concerned about family conflict (Reach Out, 2019)
- 68% of teenagers have encountered social media drama within their friend circles (Lenhart, 2015)
- 67% of teens pretend that "everything is ok" so they don't worry others, indicating severe inner conflict (National 4-H Council, 2020).

The common denominator is that teenagers fear disappointing others, being rejected, or being ridiculed. In fact, the number one fear among teenagers is the fear of rejection (Focus on the Family, 2018).

Going through life without ever experiencing conflict is impossible; however, managing conflict is achievable and something anybody can overcome with patience, practice, and perseverance.

THE NATURE OF CONFLICT

Think of conflict as an intense tug-of-war battle. People pull the rope in opposite directions based on their viewpoint, making it difficult to find common ground. When we experience conflict or disagreement, we tend to stubbornly stick to our perspective, ignoring the viewpoints of others, ultimately creating tension between us.

As tension rises and conflict intensifies, we become more determined to defend our stance on the matter and completely discredit the other side of the argument. In essence, conflict causes us to overlook the complexities of the matter and the perspectives of others involved (Bowman, 2000).

WHAT CAUSES CONFLICT?

That's a tricky one because there is no correct answer to what constitutes a conflict and what doesn't; nevertheless, shared factors commonly lead to conflicts among teenagers.

Communication Issues

Poor listening and ineffective communication can lead to misunderstandings, misinterpretations, and assumptions that could easily evolve into conflict.

Peer Pressure

Many teens face pressure to conform to certain behaviors, opinions, and social norms that they may not necessarily want to but feel obliged to in order to fit in. This can lead to conflict both internally and externally.

Conflict Of Identity

Conflict doesn't always have to be with somebody else; you can have conflicting options and thoughts about yourself. Teenagers are in a period of constant self-discovery and grapple regularly with questions related to their identity, values, and beliefs. The confusion and frustration of not being completely sure of who you are can lead to internal conflict.

Parental Expectation

When there is a difference in values, desires, and expectations between children and their parents, disagreements become far more likely, and conflict follows.

School-Related Stress

The constant need to excel academically and compete with your classmates for grades and social acceptance can contribute to conflict. These pressures may leave teenagers feeling overwhelmed with expectations, leading to frustration and tension.

Puberty

Like it or not, teenagers are going through the most drastic hormonal change they will ever experience. These changes often lead to mood swings, emotional volatility, and unfortunate combinations that create the perfect conditions for conflict to arise.

Romantic Relationships

As you explore the complexities of romantic connections for the first time, you are introduced to a host of challenges: jealousy, misunderstandings, disagreements, and boundaries. Because this is all so new to us as teenagers, we often don't know how to deal with them appropriately, and thus, conflict is born.

HEALTHY VS. UNHEALTHY CONFLICT

Conflict can be healthy and unhealthy, depending on how we approach it. Unhealthy conflict can be understood as approaching disagreement with an adversarial mindset. This is when we view one another as adversaries. When we approach conflict from a "you vs. me" perspective, we cultivate a culture of blame, prioritizing personal triumph over resolving the issue at hand.

In contrast, healthy conflict occurs when we view issues as challenges that can be overcome by jointly addressing the issue at hand. Instead of a "You vs. Me" mindset, we adopt a "You + Me vs. The Problem" perspective. This new perspective helps promote a cooperative atmosphere and mutual respect to regain normalcy in a relationship and overcome challenges (Osmani, 2023).

The differences between healthy and unhealthy conflict can be illustrated as follows:

Healthy conflict	Unhealthy conflict
Individuals focus on the issue at hand and look for solutions without feeling personally attacked or digressing to unrelated issues	Individuals prioritize self-defense and are more concerned with proving they are right than they are with understanding other perspectives to solve the problem.
Active listening is utilized	View opposing views as a personal attack and veer away from dealing with the core issue.
Feedback is prioritized to help overcome the problem together	Frustration, anger, and resentment are common
Although there may be disagreement, there is still respect for others	The conflict typically ends without any sustainable resolution. Tension remains.

Healthy Conflict: Classmates engage in respectful dialogue despite differing opinions. The group considers each perspective to collaboratively resolve the issue by working together and compromising to overcome the project-related challenge.

Unhealthy Conflict: David and Sarah recently started dating and got into an argument about their relationship. David feels like Sarah is hiding something from him because he won't let her see her phone. David launches personal attacks directed at Sarah and accuses Sarah of cheating without evidence to back it up. Sarah, on the other hand, says that it is an invasion of privacy. Ultimately, David gets upset and storms off.

STAYING CALM DURING DISAGREEMENTS AND EXPRESSING YOUR FEELINGS CONSTRUCTIVELY

In heated arguments, the most important thing we can do is remain calm, even when we feel like somebody is attacking us. When we maintain our composure, we prevent mutual hurt feelings, salvage precious relationships, and foster an environment of respect for each other.

To maintain a sense of calm in these situations, take deep breaths and ensure a longer exhale than an inhale. Understand that individuals are often angry and frustrated about external circumstances, and their emotions are not always directed at them. Once again, utilize active listening to reflect and understand what their concerns are; this will help us refrain from acting emotionally before hearing others out. Validate their emotions by expressing that you recognize they are emotional (angry or frustrated). Verbalizing their feelings illustrates genuine understanding and helps build a connection. If all else fails, request a break before you lose your composure and act emotionally; you can always come back later and pick up where you left off (Malan, 2022).

Once you have found your sense of calm, the next step is to articulate your feelings and thoughts. You also need time to be heard. To express our feelings constructively during a conflict situation, we need to remain calm, respectful, and assertive. Being assertive does not mean blaming or accusing others; instead, it means sharing our perspectives and how this situation is impacting you. Make use of "I" statements: "I think...", "I feel...", "I want...", "I need..." This technique helps us to express our emotions without assigning blame to others. "I" statements are essential to foster understanding and create a safe, open space for constructive dialogue and empathy (LinkedIn, 2023).

ROLE-PLAYING TIME

These role-playing examples are designed to present you with a potential conflict that you and a partner need to solve by working together:

Scenario 1:

Cindy posted a picture of herself at the beach on the weekend with a group of friends. However, Rachel asked if she wanted to hang out with her that weekend, and Cindy responded, "Sorry, but I need to study for the upcoming math test." This resulted in an argument the next day at school. Play the roles of Cindy and Rachel and encourage them to engage in a dialogue, focusing on active listening, empathy, and understanding without getting emotional, blaming one another, or putting one another down.

Scenario 2:

16-year-old Jessica wants to extend her curfew so that she can attend a late-night birthday party with her friends, but her parents are worried about her safety and whether she will make the right decisions at the party. Play the role of Jessica and her parents and come up with a way to diffuse the conflict through compromise.

CONFLICT RESOLUTION SKILLS

Conflict can be stressful but can also be viewed as an important opportunity for growth. Throughout my years, I have witnessed the intense emotions that can arise from conflict, but at the same time, I have also witnessed how resolving conflict in a constructive manner can improve self-awareness, enhance our communication skills, elevate problem-solving abilities, and improve our relationships.

When we avoid conflict or deal with it by adopting an aggressive approach, we undermine our relationship and create an environment where resentment thrives.

Use conflict as an opportunity to gain insights about ourselves and others, and see it as neither inherently wrong nor indicative of failure, but something that is part of the inevitable human experience.

When conflict arises, consider these five steps to shape your response:

Step One: Acknowledge the Conflict

Avoid taking the easy road and ignoring conflict. Address the issue promptly to prevent the conflict from escalating. Ignoring conflict will only lead to two outcomes. The first solution to the problem will not be found. Second, if we leave it for to long, it will become to big for us to handle when we eventually come around to resolve the problem.

Step Two: Define the Problem

What is the root cause of the conflict? Ensure you and whoever else is involved agree on the issue and discuss the unmet needs on both sides in a respectful and calm manner. Make sure you keep the discussion focused on the defined problem and avoid getting caught up with past events or personal emotions.

Step Three: Meet on Neutral Ground

When you decide to confront the issue, choose a safe, neutral environment conducive to honest communication. Meet in the middle; don't meet up somewhere close by to you but not to them, or vice versa, as this could imply that one person holds more influence or power over the other.

Step Four: Let Everyone Have a Say

Make sure all parties get an equal opportunity to express their feelings and views. If necessary, establish some ground rules to make this process run smoother. Listen to what someone else has to say before you respond. When it's your turn to speak, be calm, respectful, and assertive.

Step Five: You Don't Have to Be Proven Right

This isn't a competition; you don't always need to be right. Instead, evaluate the conflict objectively and consider taking specific actions rather than choosing a side. Don't be afraid to be the first to apologize if need be, and ask how you can resolve the issue together through mutual understanding and ensuring both your needs are met (CTRI, 2017).

Step Six: Agree on a Solution

After you have both had a chance to speak and you have considered both perspectives, determine the most favorable solution for everybody involved. Explore the underlying source of the conflict, learn from it, and avoid premature judgments before considering the proposed solution.

Step Seven: Determine Each Side's Role in the Solution

Make sure all parties find the solution to be fair. Utilize open dialogue to cultivate mutual understanding and agree on what each of you needs to do to resolve the conflict. Work collaboratively to establish steps toward achieving the agreed-upon resolution (Herrity, 2023).

THE IMPORTANCE OF EMPATHY

When it comes to conflict resolution, empathy is our secret weapon. It helps to prevent assumptions, judgments, and biases that ultimately complicate issues. Beyond that, it minimizes negative emotions like fear, jealousy, and anger and influences clear thinking, problem-solving skills, and better decision-making. Being more empathetic in high-tension situations promotes a positive and respectful atmosphere where everybody can be heard and valued. Empathy is the perfect recipe for a win-win solution (LinkedIn, 2023b).

FINDING WIN-WIN SOLUTIONS

A win-win relationship prioritizes mutual benefit and nurtures a culture of shared success. It thrives on cooperation, compromise, collaboration, and mutual understanding, diverging from zero-sum dynamics (one's gain equals another's loss). It is an approach that lays a robust foundation for healthy connections through fostering respect, empathy, and consideration.

In a win-win solution, empathy helps us to anticipate and address other's needs; active listening showcases interest; and working towards a common goal and compromise helps drive us toward finding balanced solutions and a common purpose. Finally, showing appreciation towards others reinforces positivity and enables us to acknowledge contributions.

A win-win solution is always the solution to strive for when resolving conflict, as it showcases our commitment to understanding, collaborating, and mutual growth, paving the way to reinforce relationships that can stand the test of time (Trujillo, 2023).

APOLOGIZING AND FORGIVING

Apologies have the potential to mend wounds when they are sincere, and although they may be tough at times, they are essential to maintaining healthy relationships. The reality is that an apology encompasses more than mere words. Saying, "I'm sorry" is one thing, but it is through our actions that we show sincerity.

Furthermore, a sincere apology can reshape past events and effectively resolve conflict. They provide the apologizer with the opportunity to acknowledge their feelings of guilt and understand the impact their actions have on those around them. When delivered with sincerity, apologies are potent catalysts for effective conflict resolution. (Otting, 2023).

EXERCISE: CONFLICT LOTTERY

For this exercise, you or a friend will write 10–15 conflict scenarios and put them in a hat. You will then draw one of the conflict scenarios from the hat at random. Once you have the scenario, you will have 5 minutes to jot down as many solutions to that proposed scenario as possible. Once time is up, you will categorize which solutions are healthy or unhealthy.

If you have more unhealthy than healthy solutions, then you know you need to work on your conflict resolution skills. In fact, even if your solutions are approximately half healthy and half unhealthy, you could still improve your conflict resolution skills. The aim of this exercise is to try and find healthier solutions than unhealthy solutions and test your ability to resolve conflict and find win-win solutions.

NAVIGATING REJECTION

Rejection. It's a word that strikes fear in the hearts of the majority of the population. Often, rejection immediately shrouds people with feelings of discomfort, unworthiness, and self-doubt. The sting of rejection transcends the physical realm; it is a pain that leaves a lasting imprint on our psyche and is not just a fear but a mindset. If left to its own devices, fear of rejection can shape our interactions with the world, influence our relationships, shatter our self-esteem, and break down our confidence. In a nutshell, fear of rejection is the perceived risk of not being accepted by others and being hurt as a result. It is linked to our belief that we are not able to meet other's expectations. It becomes like a self-fulfilling prophecy. If we give into the belief that we are not good enough before we have even tried, self-doubt and self-criticism will intensify.

Fear of rejection can be extremely toxic and self-sabotaging, leading to a myriad of symptoms.

- Becoming excessively self-conscious and anxious about everyday social situations
- Needing constant reassurance and seeking the approval of others to alleviate fear of perceived inadequacy
- Avoiding trying new experiences or dabbling in activities due to the fear of messing up or potential embarrassment
- Engaging in negative self-talk, leading to poor self-belief
- Becoming overly sensitive to criticism by taking it personally and viewing it as an affront
- Struggling to make and maintain relationships due to the underlying fear of rejection

HOW TO PROCESS AND COPE WITH REJECTION

Rejection stings; we've all been there. What's important is finding healthy ways to process and cope with rejection. By adopting effective strategies to boost our confidence and find the strength within, this challenging process can become easier to manage. Being honest with ourselves, self-reflecting, planning for the future, and assessing a situation rationally and not emotionally are the weapons at our disposal to overcome rejection and grow as individuals.

Following these steps can help us cope with rejection and overcome the challenges it brings:

Step One: Acknowledge and Accept Rejection

First and foremost, we need to accept that rejection is often situational. We cannot allow ourselves to internalize it as a reflection of our self-worth. Understanding rejection in context and accepting that it is part of life is the first step to managing rejection effectively.

Step Two: Process Your Emotions Thoughtfully

Once we grasp this key first step, we need to reflect on what we are feeling. List each emotion you are feeling and understand why you are feeling that way. Through this acknowledgment, we are able to regroup and cope with our emotions more constructively.

Step Three: Seek Feedback and Emotional Support

If you are still unsure about your feelings, don't be afraid to seek constructive feedback from others, as they may offer the valuable insights you need to grow and improve yourself. Don't ignore your support system; lean on them for the emotional support you need during challenging times in your life. Not only will this help provide comfort, but you will also learn from diverse perspectives to cope with rejection.

Step Four: Refrain From Indulging Negative Self-Talk

Change your outlook from self-criticism to self-acceptance; being hurtful towards yourself will only leave you feeling worse and limit your growth. Practice self-compassion by focusing on your unique strengths, not your weaknesses.

Step Five: Reframe the Situation

Reflect on the bigger picture at hand and understand that things often work out just how they were meant to, even if it doesn't seem so at the time. Rejection is an opportunity to grow as much as it is a setback. Shift the blame away from yourself and consider a more rational perspective. For instance, if you ask a girl out who you really like and they reject you because they aren't ready to commit to a relationship, it will be disheartening at first. However, this is not a reflection of your worth or desirability. Instead of blaming yourself, see it as an opportunity to focus on exploring other interests and allow both of you the time and space to mature and self-improve before pursuing a committed relationship.

Step Six: Plan Ahead and Remember This is Not the End

Identify areas where you can grow, generate a plan of action, stick with it to navigate future challenges, and dust yourself off after disappointment. Build resilience in the face of rejection by adopting a positive mindset, being adaptable to changing circumstances beyond your control, persisting despite failing, becoming more self-aware, and finding strength in your dependable support system (Hickson, 2023).

The Importance of Self-Worth Goes Beyond Others' Opinions

In the face of self-doubt, we often rely on external sources of validation to help navigate our uncertainties. We seek this validation from our friends, family, peers, authority figures, and anyone we respect and trust.

While receiving that validation, may feel great in the moment, relying on it extensively overshadows our need for competence and autonomy, thus having a detrimental effect on our self-worth in the long run.

Relying solely on validation from others creates a cycle of chasing success so that we can prove our worth to others but not ourselves. This results in a never-ending quest for reassurance. However, we can break free from this cycle if we recognize that our self-worth is not tied to our achievements, but rather to how comfortable we feel within ourselves and our willingness to give ourselves praise for doing our best. Shifting our perspective towards intrinsic self-worth, which is independent of external validation, opinions, or judgments, is incredibly liberating and fosters genuine fulfillment within ourselves and satisfaction with our capabilities (Gervais, 2024).

Messi Overcame Rejection to Become the G.O.A.T of Soccer

At the age of 11, Lionel Messi faced rejection from his local soccer club as he was deemed to be too short to play the game due to a hormone deficiency. This ultimately led his childhood club to drop him from the team.

However, Messi did not let this rejection define him and got hormonal treatment to aid in his growth, although even with the treatments, he only stood at 5, 7". He managed to make it professionally, but even at 5'7", he had many skeptics who doubted his potential. Yet, Messi wasn't deterred. Through resilience, he silenced the doubters by shattering numerous records, winning a World Cup, and winning countless club trophies. He would also go on to clinch eight Ballon d'Or (the highest individual accolade in world soccer), surpassing any other player by a remarkable three victories for this trophy. Messi was well aware of his small stature, but he shrugged off his weakness by working on his explosive abilities on the field to defy limitations.

Messi's story showcases how setbacks do not define us and that, through resilience and determination, we can achieve success beyond our wildest imaginations.

Now that we have navigated the challenges of conflict and rejection, let's reflect on our journey thus far, and march forward to become our best selves!

EMPOWER TEENS WITH CONFIDENCE

Inspire Growth and Happiness

Self-confidence is the key to unlocking new opportunities. Did you know that spreading kindness and support can lead to happiness and success? Help us make a difference!

Would you extend a helping hand to someone in need, even anonymously? Picture a teenager much like you once were, seeking guidance to navigate life's challenges.

Our mission is to place "Self-confidence For Teens" in the hands of every teenager. Your support can make this happen.

Could you spare a minute to write a review for this book? Your words can empower teens to:

- Feel supported in their community
- Take brave steps toward their dreams
- Express themselves meaningfully
- Overcome challenges
- See their dreams come true

Simply scan the QR code to leave your review at the link provided.

If helping teens navigate social challenges resonates with you, you're in good company. Join us in making a positive impact.

Excited to help you boost your confidence and mental health with the upcoming chapters. Thank you for your support!

Your cheerleader, Aubrey Andrus

PS: Sharing something valuable not only benefits others but also increases your value in their eyes. Spread joy by sharing this book with someone who could use it!

CONCLUSION

As we stand tall take a moment to reflect on just how far we have come. We've embraced the influence of positive daily habits, confronted and managed fears and anxieties, mastered confident communication, responsibly navigated the digital realm, fortified resilience, set our sights on growth-oriented goals, delved into the depths of our identities, cultivated healthy relationships, and learned to handle conflict and rejection with unwavering determination.

These insights are essential for our growth and define who we are, helping us shape our teenage years to reflect the people we desire to become in the future. Adopting positive habits is the bedrock for sustainable and desired growth while learning to manage stress and anxiety is essential to navigating obstacles in our way and overcoming challenges. Through mastering the art of confident communication and adopting responsible use of social media platforms, we have become far more adept at navigating personal and digital interactions.

Building our resilience has empowered us to see challenges as opportunities and handle them with grace when life throws a storm our way. Setting SMART goals launches us forward to stay committed to our personal development and realization of our dreams. By becoming more self-aware, we can be authentically ourselves and know ourselves better than before, helping us build healthy relationships embedded in mutual respect and understanding and forming the foundation of a fulfilling life.

Throughout this dynamic journey, we have come to realize that self-development, self-confidence, and self-discovery are not static destinations but journeys we are always taking. To continually become better versions of ourselves, we need to be persistent and adopt an eagerness to learn, in addition to having an unwavering commitment to evolve as individuals. Everything we do in our daily lives has a purpose, from the daily habits we cultivate to our interactions with others, the goals we set, how we manage our stress, and how we overcome challenges, which contribute to the mosaic of our very essence, confidence, and empowerment.

Armed with this knowledge, it is up to you, my wonderful readers, to transform these strategies and insights from understanding to action. The power to shape our futures with confidence exists in all of us, and through consistently working on ourselves and putting these lessons into action, you can become the confident and determined individual you desire. Do not consider this the conclusion of our journey, but rather an invitation to put everything you have learned into practice and reap the fruits of your effort. Learn from every experience, celebrate every achievement, and let setbacks be catalysts for growth.

Before I bid you all farewell, I want to leave you all with one of my favorite quotes. It is simple, but few truer words have ever been spoken. "Believe you can, and you're halfway there." These were the wise words of Theodore Roosevelt. May they light a fire in you like they have for me. May your journey be as extraordinary as the exceptional individual you are. I wish you all the best!

REFERENCES

Ackerman, C. E. (2019, May 27). *49 Communication Activities, Exercises & Games.* PositivePsychology.com. https://positivepsychology.com/communication-games-and-activities/#relationship

Alangui, M. (2022, February 8). *12 Small Habits That Can Lead To Big Changes.* Www.linkedin.com. https://www.linkedin.com/pulse/12-small-habits-can-lead-big-changes-mari-alangui/

Allo Health. (2023, July 4). *The Importance Of Mutual Respect In A Relationship | Allo Health.* Www.allohealth.care. https://www.allohealth.care/healthfeed/sex-educa tion/mutual-respect-in-a-relationship

AlSabbah, H. (2020, September 27). *The Biggest Influences On Our Identities.* The Biggest Influences on Our Identities. https://medium.com/the-biggest-influ ences-on-our-identities/the-biggest-influences-on-our-identities-b78654b79d43

American Psychological Association. (2022). *What is exposure therapy?* Apa.org. https://www.apa.org/ptsd-guideline/patients-and-families/exposure-therapy#:

Back on Track Teens. (2021, April 2). *Find your voice to release your own personal power.* Back on Track Teens. https://www.backontrackteens.com/blog/find-voice-release-personal-power/

Bacon, N. (2020, October 1). *How Values Affect Decision Making.* Mom on Purpose. https://momonpurpose.com/how-values-affect-decision-making/

Batra, D. (2019, May 25). *Your belief shapes your reality.* Www.linkedin.com. https://www.linkedin.com/pulse/your-belief-shapes-reality-divya-dhingra/

Bechler, J. (2022, April 7). *Strikeout King.* Jamy Bechler. partshttps://jamybechler.com/strikeout-king/?

Better Help. (2024, January 30). *The Importance of Setting Boundaries: 10 Benefits for You and Your Relationships | BetterHelp.* Www.betterhelp.com. https://www.better help.com/advice/general/the-importance-of-setting-boundaries-10-benefits-for-you-and-your-relationships/

Bizga, alina. (2022, March 9). *Think Before You Post: Creating a Positive Digital Footprint and Why It Matters.* Hot for Security. https://www.bitdefender.com/blog/hotforsecurity/think-before-you-post-creating-a-positive-digital-footprint-and-why-it-matters/

Boogaard, K. (2021, December 26). *How to write SMART goals.* Work Life by

Atlassian. https://www.atlassian.com/blog/productivity/how-to-write-smart-goals#:

Bowman, K. (2000). *Conflict resolution* (pp. 5–6). chrome-extension://efaidnbmnnnibpcajpcglclefindmkaj/https://www.cpd.utoronto.ca/endoflife/Modules/CONFLICT%20RESOLUTION%20MODULE.pdf

Bradley, J. (2023, June 25). *Self-Confidence and Decision-Making: Trusting Yourself.* Lampshade of ILLUMINATION. https://medium.com/lampshade-of-illumination/self-confidence-and-decision-making-trusting-yourself-82b5eb8bf1df

British Heart Foundation. (2018, May 14). *Active listening.* British Heart Foundation. https://www.bhf.org.uk/informationsupport/heart-matters-magazine/wellbeing/how-to-talk-about-health-problems/active-listening

Brower, T. (2023, September 24). *For Pay, Productivity And Wellbeing, Data Points To The Power Of Exercise.* Forbes. https://www.forbes.com/sites/tracybrower/2023/09/24/for-pay-productivity-and-wellbeing-data-points-to-the-power-of-exercise/?sh=e8b999c561c6

Brown, L. (2023, May 24). *12 signs you're in a relationship with a genuinely supportive partner.* Hack Spirit. https://hackspirit.com/relationship-with-supportive-partner/

Buckloh, L. (2018). *5 Ways to Know Your Feelings Better (for Teens) - KidsHealth.* Kidshealth.org. https://kidshealth.org/en/teens/emotional-awareness.html

Calm. (2023a, September 12). *5, 4, 3, 2, 1 — a simple grounding exercise to calm anxiety.* Calm Blog. https://www.calm.com/blog/5-4-3-2-1-a-simple-exercise-to-calm-the-mind#:

Calm. (2023b, November 16). *How to overcome fear of change: 8 ways to navigate the unknown.* Calm Blog. https://www.calm.com/blog/fear-of-change

Calm. (2024, January 5). *Reframing negative thoughts: how to challenge negative thinking.* Calm Blog. https://www.calm.com/blog/reframing-negative-thoughts

Campbell, F. (2019, February 13). *Using Curiosity To Find Your Best Self.* Www.stackery.iousing-Curiosity. https://www.stackery.io/blog/using-curiosity/

Center for Parent and Teen Communication. (2022, September 4). *Ways for Teens to Tackle Problems.* Center for Parent and Teen Communication. https://parentandteen.com/stress-management-for-teens-identify-and-then-tackle-the-problem/

Cherry, K. (2023a, February 23). *Understanding Body Language and Facial Expressions.* Verywell Mind. https://www.verywellmind.com/understand-body-language-and-facial-expressions-4147228

Cherry, K. (2023b, May 3). *Motivation: Psychological factors that guide behavior.* Verywell Mind. https://www.verywellmind.com/what-is-motivation-2795378

Christian, L. (2021, November 16). *How to Focus on What You Can Control (and Win More Battles).* SoulSalt. https://soulsalt.com/focus-on-what-you-can-control/

Connolly, M. (2020, May 13). *4 Core Components of Resilience: How To Become A More*

Resilient Person. Neways Somatic Psychotherapy & Coaching. https://newayscen ter.com/components-of-resilience-become-resilient-person/

Cooks-Campbell, A. (2022, July 22). *The subtle, but important, difference between confidence and arrogance*. Www.betterup.com. https://www.betterup.com/blog/confi dence-vs-arrogance

CTRI. (2017, May 11). *5 Steps For Effective Conflict Resolution - Crisis & Trauma Resource Institute*. Ctrinstitute.com. https://ctrinstitute.com/blog/effective-conflict-resolution/

Cumberland, D. (2020, July 1). *The Secret To Finding Your Voice*. Themeaningmovement.com. https://themeaningmovement.com/finding-your-voice/

Daisie. (2023, July 18). *Building Resilience: Overcoming Rejection and Bouncing Back*. Daisie Blog. https://blog.daisie.com/building-resilience-overcoming-rejection-and-bouncing-back/

DK, S. (2023, August 29). *Share Your Passion with Others: Spread the Joy and Inspire!* Medium. https://medium.com/@sandeepsunil01/share-your-passion-with-others-spread-the-joy-and-inspire-2c90d21f758b

Do Something. (2019). *11 Facts about Cyber Bullying* . Dosomething.org; Dosomething.org. https://www.dosomething.org/us/facts/11-facts-about-cyber-bullying

Dowches-Wheeler, J. (2023, February 20). *7 Questions to Ask to Discover Your Passion*. Bright Space Coaching | Leadership Development for Women. https://www.brightspacecoaching.com/blog/find-your-passion

Eatough, E. (2021, July 15). *How to set goals and achieve them: 10 strategies for success*. Better Up. https://www.betterup.com/blog/how-to-set-goals-and-achieve-them

Everyday Design . (2022, February 18). *FAQ: How can you break down large goals into smaller, more manageable steps? - Everyday Design*. Www.everyday.design. https://www.everyday.design/faqs/how-can-you-break-down-large-goals-into-smaller-more-manageable-steps#:

Faster Capital. (2022, November 1). *Honest: The Art of Honesty: Building Trust in Relationships*. Faster Capital. https://fastercapital.com/content/Honest--The-Art-of-Honesty--Building-Trust-in-Relationships.html

Fearless. (2023, February 6). *The Benefits of Starting the Day Positively on Your Mental and Physical Health – FearLess*. Fearless. https://fearless.org.au/2023/02/06/the-benefits-of-starting-the-day-positively-on-your-mental-and-physical-health/#:

Focus on the Family. (2018, November 14). *3 Things Your Teens Fear the Most*. Focus on the Family. https://www.focusonthefamily.com/parenting/3-things-your-teens-fear-the-most/

Gasparinetti, F. (2023, April 10). *The Importance of Celebrating Small Wins*. Www.linkedin.com. https://www.linkedin.com/pulse/importance-celebrating-small-wins-francesco-gasparinetti

Gervais, M. (2024, February 16). *Stop Basing Your Self-Worth on Other People's Opinions*. Harvard Business Review. https://hbr.org/2024/02/stop-basing-your-self-worth-on-other-peoples-opinions

Grade University. (2023, February 21). *10 activities for developing listening skills*. Grade-University.com. https://grade-university.com/blog/10-activities-for-developing-listening-skills

GRIN. (2018). *12 Kid Influencers That Can Help You Target the Younger Generation | | GRIN - Influencer Marketing Software*. Grin.co. https://grin.co/blog/kid-influencers/

Gupta, S. (2022, November 14). *How to Respect Other People's Boundaries*. Verywell Mind. https://www.verywellmind.com/how-to-respect-other-peoples-bound aries-6824706

Harvard. (2021, August 14). *Giving thanks can make you happier*. Harvard Health. https://www.health.harvard.edu/healthbeat/giving-thanks-can-make-you-happier#:

Hasa. (2020, November 2). *What is the Difference Between Hobby and Passion*. Pediaa.com. https://pediaa.com/what-is-the-difference-between-hobby-and-passion/

Healthdirect Australia. (2022, October 19). *Motivation: How to get started and staying motivated*. Www.healthdirect.gov.au. https://www.healthdirect.gov.au/motiva tion-how-to-get-started-and-staying-motivated#:

Healthline. (2022, July 28). *The 333 Rule for Anxiety and Other Coping Strategies*. Healthline. https://www.healthline.com/health/333-rule-anxiety#other-coping-strategies

Herrity, J. (2023, July 31). *5 effective conflict resolution strategies*. Indeed Career Guide. https://www.indeed.com/career-advice/career-development/conflict-resolu tion-strategies

Hesler, B. (2023, February 21). *5 tips to manage stress*. Mayo Clinic Health System. https://www.mayoclinichealthsystem.org/hometown-health/speaking-of-health/5-tips-to-manage-stress

Hickey, C. (2019, January 11). *The Dos and Don'ts of Being a Supportive Friend*. MyTherapyNYC - Counseling & Wellness. https://mytherapynyc.com/being-a-supportive-friend/#:

Hickson, J. (2023, October 2). *How to Deal With Rejection: 10 Ways to Move On*. Choosing Therapy. https://www.choosingtherapy.com/deal-with-rejection/

Hudson, A. (2022, November 21). *9 Reasons Why Your Teenager Doesn't Want To Talk → Here is What To Do*. Ashley Hudson LMFT. https://www.ashleyhudsontherapy.com/post/9-reasons-why-your-teenager-doesnt-want-to-talk#:

Iliades, C. (2018, January 5). *Photo Gallery: 7 Anxiety-Attack Triggers*.

EverydayHealth.com.   https://www.everydayhealth.com/anxiety-pictures/7-surprising-causes-of-anxiety.aspx

Incoc. (2021, April 22). *Analogies.* Www.incoc.org. https://www.incoc.org/Resources/Analogies.asp?Qid=26

Indeed. (2023, October 23). *Empathic Listening: Definition, Examples and Tips.* Indeed Career Guide. https://www.indeed.com/career-advice/career-development/empathic-listening#:

Inspire Speakers. (2020, January 2). *Jessica Watson | Inspire Speakers.* Www.inspirespeakers.com.au.   https://www.inspirespeakers.com.au/speakers/show/jessica-watson/

Jayson Darby. (2022, November 1). *What Are the Big 5 Personality Traits?* Thomas International. https://www.thomas.co/resources/type/hr-guides/what-are-big-5-personality-traits

Johal, S. (2020, July 30). *Bouncing Back: 6 Stories of Triumph after Rejection.* Www.linkedin.com. https://www.linkedin.com/pulse/bouncing-back-6-stories-triumph-after-rejection-shawn-johal/

Leal, C. J. (2021, January 28). *Kanban Zone.* Kanban Zone - Visual Collaboration for Lean and Agile Portfolio Project Management. https://kanbanzone.com/2021/how-to-break-down-tasks-into-smaller-ones/

LeClair, C. (2023, February 6). *Communicating Boundaries.* Www.linkedin.com. https://www.linkedin.com/pulse/communicating-boundaries-cassandra-leclair-ph-d-/

Lenhart, A. (2015, August 6). *Chapter 5: Conflict, Friendships and Technology.* Pew Research Center: Internet, Science & Tech; Pew Research Center: Internet, Science & Tech. https://www.pewresearch.org/internet/2015/08/06/chapter-5-conflict-friendships-and-technology/

Lewis , J. (2023, July 11). *The Root of Rejection Fear and Its Impact on Self-esteem.* Www.zellalife.com. https://www.zellalife.com/blog/rejection-fear/

LinkedIn. (2023a, November 11). *What are some effective strategies to handle emotions in conflict situations?* Www.linkedin.com. https://www.linkedin.com/advice/0/what-some-effective-strategies-handle-emotions

LinkedIn. (2023b, December 1). *How can empathy help you resolve conflicts in the workplace?* Www.linkedin.com. https://www.linkedin.com/advice/0/how-can-empathy-help-you-resolve-conflicts#:

Liu, Q., Jiang, M., Li, S., & Yang, Y. (2021). Social support, resilience, and self-esteem protect against common mental health problems in early adolescence. *Medicine, 100*(4). https://doi.org/10.1097/md.0000000000024334

Malan, M. (2022, February 16). *6 Tools To Remain Calm During A Heated Argument.* Medium. https://medium.com/@monikamalan/6-tools-to-remain-calm-during-a-heated-argument-90ca26095c4f

Marr, B. (2014, October 27). *How to Start a Conversation with Absolutely Anyone.* Www.linkedin.com. https://www.linkedin.com/pulse/20141027073838-64875646-how-to-start-a-conversation-with-absolutely-anyone/

Marteka. (2019, July 15). *12 Ways to Recognise Negative Thoughts.* Benevolent Health. https://benevolenthealth.co.uk/12-ways-to-recognise-negative-thoughts/

MasterClass. (2022, May 13). *Making a Mistake: How to Learn From Mistakes.* MasterClass. https://www.masterclass.com/articles/making-a-mistake

Mayo Clinic. (2020a, August 18). *Exercise and stress: Get moving to manage stress.* Mayo Clinic. https://www.mayoclinic.org/healthy-lifestyle/stress-management/in-depth/exercise-and-stress/art-20044469#:

Mayo Clinic. (2020b, October 27). *How to Build Resiliency.* Mayo Clinic. https://www.mayoclinic.org/tests-procedures/resilience-training/in-depth/resilience/art-20046311

Mclean Hospital. (2023, August 27). *Understanding Fear, Anxiety, and Phobias | McLean Hospital.* Www.mcleanhospital.org. https://www.mcleanhospital.org/essential/fear-phobias#:

Millen, J. (2022, July 12). *How to Challenge Your Beliefs.* Www.johnmillen.com. https://www.johnmillen.com/blog/challenge-your-beliefs

Mind Tools. (2023, May 26). *MindTools | Home.* Www.mindtools.com. https://www.mindtools.com/air49f4/using-affirmations#:

Mind Tools . (2022a). *Active Listening.* Www.mindtools.com. https://www.mindtools.com/az4wxv7/active-listening

Mind Tools . (2022b). *What Are Your Values?* Mind Tools. https://www.mindtools.com/a5eygum/what-are-your-values

Mind Tools Content Team. (2023). *MindTools | Home.* Www.mindtools.com. https://www.mindtools.com/a5ycdws/visualization

Mindful Teachers. (2023, April 23). *5 Mindfulness Exercises for Teens.* Mindful Teachers. https://www.mindfulteachers.org/blog/mindfulness-exercises-for-teens

Morning Coach. (2022, October 7). *Identifying What Matters to You.* Www.morningcoach.com. https://www.morningcoach.com/blog/identifying-what-matters-to-you

My Kids Vision. (2022). *Screen time in teenagers: how can we manage it? | My Kids Vision.* Www.mykidsvision.org. https://www.mykidsvision.org/knowledge-centre/screen-time-in-teenagers-how-can-we-manage-it#:

National 4-H.Council. (2020, June 17). *New Survey Finds 7 in 10 Teens Are Struggling with Mental Health.* Www.prnewswire.com. https://www.prnewswire.com/news-releases/new-survey-finds-7-in-10-teens-are-struggling-with-mental-health-301078336.html

Neff, K. D. (2009). The role of self-compassion in development: A healthier way to relate to oneself. *Human Development, 52*(4), 211–214. https://doi.org/10.1159/000215071

Nemours Kids Health. (2024, January 9). *Cyberbullying (for Parents) - Nemours KidsHealth.* Kidshealth.org. https://kidshealth.org/en/parents/cyberbullying.html#:

North, T. (2023, February 1). *The 12 Benefits of Increasing Your Self-Confidence.* Www.tcnorth.com. https://www.tcnorth.com/building-confidence/12-benefits-increasing-self-confidence/#:

Occo London. (2023, February 1). *How to Keep Multiple Interests In Balance and Achieve Success.* OCCO London. https://www.occolondon.com/blogs/learn/multipassionate#:

Osmani, A. (2023, July 16). *Unhealthy conflict vs. healthy conflict.* Addyosmani.com. https://addyosmani.com/blog/healthy-unhealthy-conflict/#:

Otting, K. (2023, February 8). *Articles.* Interaction Management Associates. https://imamediation.com/blog/why-an-apology-can-be-a-powerful-catalyst-for-conflict-resolution#:

People Builders. (2022, June 10). *Overcoming Life's Challenges with Resilience | People Builders.* Www.peoplebuilders.com.au. https://www.peoplebuilders.com.au/blog/overcoming-lifes-challenges-with-resilience#:

Perry, E. (2022, December 11). *Self-Reflection: What Does It Mean & How to Self-Reflect.* Www.betterup.com. https://www.betterup.com/blog/self-reflection#:

Peterson , T. J. (2023, November 12). *What Is Self-Confidence? | HealthyPlace.* Www.healthyplace.com. https://www.healthyplace.com/self-help/self-confidence/what-is-self-confidence

Positivity Guides . (2022, June 2). *6 Healthy Outlets For Difficult Emotions - Positivity Guides.* Positivity Guides. https://www.positivityguides.net/6-healthy-outlets-for-difficult-emotions/

Prasad, A. (2015, November 28). *8 Steps for Embracing Your Uniqueness - Dr. Asha Prasad.* Dr. Asha. https://drashaprasad.com/self-awareness/embrace-your-uniqueness/

Project Red Ribbon. (2013, August 1). *What is the Biggest Influence on Self Esteem During Puberty.* Www.linkedin.com. https://www.linkedin.com/pulse/what-biggest-influence-self-esteem-during-puberty/

Psych Central. (2015, April 12). *5 Tips to Improve Your Self-Talk.* Psych Central. https://psychcentral.com/blog/5-tips-to-improve-your-self-talk#1

Ratey, J. J. (2019, October 24). *Can exercise help treat anxiety?* Harvard Health Blog; Harvard Health Publishing. https://www.health.harvard.edu/blog/can-exercise-help-treat-anxiety-2019102418096

Raypole, C. (2021, May 17). *Ready, Set, Journal! 64 Journaling Prompts for Self-*

Discovery. Psych Central. https://psychcentral.com/blog/ready-set-journal-64-journaling-prompts-for-self-discovery

Razzetti, G. (2020, January 17). *What Do You Stand For? An Exercise to Discover Your Values | By Gustavo Razzetti*. Fearlessculture.design. https://www.fearlessculture.design/blog-posts/what-do-you-stand-for-an-exercise-to-discover-your-values

Reach Out. (2019). *Family conflict and teenagers - ReachOut Parents*. Reachout.com. https://parents.au.reachout.com/common-concerns/everyday-issues/family-conflict-and-teenagers

Ries, J. (2022, December 15). *How to Stop Constantly Comparing Yourself to Other People Online*. SELF. https://www.self.com/story/social-media-comparison-tips

Rissanen, V. (2022, January 5). *The 4-Step Process To Break Down ANY Goal Into Actionable Plan*. Www.linkedin.com. https://www.linkedin.com/pulse/4-step-process-break-down-any-goal-actionable-plan-cesnulyte-/

Ronin, K. (2020, June 19). *9 myths about confidence that are holding you back*. The Muse. https://www.themuse.com/advice/9-myths-about-confidence-that-are-holding-you-back

Rosen, K. (2019, March 25). *5 Listening Mistakes That Are Holding You Back*. Iammagazine . https://www.iamagazine.com/strategies/5-listening-mistakes-that-are-holding-you-back

Sacred Journeys . (2021, March 29). *The Four Cornerstones of a Healthy Relationship*. Sacred Journeys . https://www.sacredjourneys.co.za/blog/the-four-corner stones-of-a-healthy-relationship/

Scott, E. (2019). *5 Simple Steps to Assertive Communication*. Verywell Mind. https://www.verywellmind.com/learn-assertive-communication-in-five-simple-steps-3144969

Scott, E. (2022, January 25). *How to Improve Your Relationships With Effective Communication Skills*. Verywell Mind; Verywell Mind. https://www.verywell mind.com/managing-conflict-in-relationships-communication-tips-3144967

Sedona Sky Academy . (2024, January 24). *10 Common Causes of Anxiety in Teens*. Www.sedonasky.org. https://www.sedonasky.org/blog/common-causes-of-anxi ety-in-teens

Shahid, K. (2023, January 11). *11 Surprising Goal Setting Statistics To Crush 2023*. Bramework | AI Writer That Helps You Write Blogs 5X Faster. https://www.bramework.com/goal-setting-statistics/#:

Sheanoy, P. (2023). *20 Goals to Set For Yourself to Further Your Personal Development*. Indeed Career Guide. https://www.indeed.com/career-advice/career-develop ment/list-of-goals-set-for-yourself

Singh, P. (2024, January 31). *Neuroplasticity for Confidence*. Www.linkedin.com. https://www.linkedin.com/pulse/neuroplasticity-confidence-priyanka-singh-itswc/?trk=public_post_main-feed-card_feed-article-content

Skill Share . (2024, February 8). *8 Artists on Overcoming Self-Doubt*. Skill Share . https://www.skillshare.com/en/blog/8-artists-on-overcoming-self-doubt/

Star, K. (2019). *Visualization Techniques Can Help Manage Your Symptoms*. Verywell Mind. https://www.verywellmind.com/visualization-for-relaxation-2584112

Strangemore-Jones, G. (2024, January 15). *Exploring the Evidence-backed Wonders of Mindfulness for Mental and Physical Wellbeing*. Www.linkedin.com. https://www.linkedin.com/pulse/exploring-evidence-backed-wonders-mindfulness-mental-gareth-sc2ee/?trk=public_post

Suicide Call Back Service. (2023, November 12). *How to build a strong support network*. Suicide Call Back Service. https://www.suicidecallbackservice.org.au/mental-health/how-to-build-a-strong-support-network/

Syed, M. (2015, September 19). *Why Successful People Embrace Failure*. Www.linkedin.com. https://www.linkedin.com/pulse/why-successful-people-embrace-failure-matthew-syed/

The Big Red Group. (2022, July 23). *7 Tips to Improve your Public Speaking in High School*. The Big Red Group. https://www.thebigredgroup.com/7-tips-to-improve-your-public-speaking-in-high-school-ace-it-to-make-it/

Thriveworks. (2023, April 26). *What Is the 333 Rule for Anxiety | Thriveworks*. Https://Thriveworks.com/. https://thriveworks.com/help-with/anxiety/what-is-3-3-3-rule-for-anxiety/

True Sport. (2023, November). *10 Easy Ways to Build Resilience for Yourself and Your Team*. TrueSport. https://truesport.org/perseverance/build-resilience-yourself-team/

Trujilo, A. (2023, August 16). *The Power of Win-Win Relationships: Building the Foundation for Long-Term Success*. Steele Consulting Inc. https://www.steeleconsult.com/how-you-both-can-win/#:

Tutor Doctor. (2023, January 23). *Our Top Mindfulness Activities For Teens*. Tutor Doctor. https://www.tutordoctor.co.uk/blog/2021/february/our-top-mindfulness-activities-for-teens/

University of Rochester . (2022, November 12). *Understanding the Teen Brain - Health Encyclopedia - University of Rochester Medical Center*. Www.urmc.rochester.edu. https://www.urmc.rochester.edu/encyclopedia/content.aspx?ContentTypeID=1&ContentID=3051#:

University of Texas. (2020, November 3). *How Much of Communication Is Nonverbal? | UT Permian Basin Online*. Online.utpb.edu. https://online.utpb.edu/about-us/articles/communication/how-much-of-communication-is-nonverbal/#:

Webwise. (2019, September 5). *Dealing with online harassment -*. Webwise.ie. https://www.webwise.ie/trending/dealing-with-online-harassment/

Whyte, A. (2019, April 1). *Teen Stress and Anxiety: Facts and Statistics*. Evolve

Treatment Centers. https://evolvetreatment.com/blog/teen-stress-anxiety-facts/#:

Winter, C. (2013, May 21). *10 Benefits of Reading: Why You Should Read Every Day.* Lifehack; Lifehack. https://www.lifehack.org/articles/lifestyle/10-benefits-reading-why-you-should-read-everyday.html

Wooll, M. (2022, June 30). *How to Set Daily Goals: 4 Tips for Work and Everyday.* Www.betterup.com. https://www.betterup.com/blog/how-to-set-daily-goals

Yin, A. (2017, October 23). Coping With Teenage Anxiety: Readers Share Their Stories. *The New York Times.* https://www.nytimes.com/2017/10/23/magazine/coping-with-teenage-anxiety-readers-share-their-stories.html

Made in United States
Troutdale, OR
12/13/2024